ULTIMATE
Pace Secrets

Ian Pont

Mavericks Cricket Institute

ULTIMATE PACE SECRETS

Copyright © 2012 by Ian Pont

All rights reserved. No part of this publication may be reproduced, distributed, or transmitted in any form or by any means, including photocopying, recording, or other electronic or mechanical methods, without the prior written permission of the publisher, except in the case of brief quotations embodied in critical reviews and certain other noncommercial uses permitted by copyright law. For permission requests, write to the publisher, addressed "Attention: Permissions Coordinator," at the address below.

MCI
40 Cherry Tree Close
Halstead
Essex
CO9 2UA
United Kingdom
www.maverickscricket.com

Ordering Information:
Quantity sales. Special discounts are available on quantity purchases by corporations, associations, and others. For details, contact the publisher at the address above.

Please contact MCI: Tel: (44) 1787 479071

Contents

Dedication
Acknowledgement and Thanks
About The Author
Why This Book?
Introduction

1. Welcome To Russia
2. Small Keys Open Big Locks
3. Your Journey To Work
4. Jump To It
5. Technique Is Not The Most Important Thing. It's the ONLY Thing
6. The Four Tent Pegs
7. Drop Step, Front Foot Block, Stretch Reflex
8. Not So Simple Forces At Play, Made Easy
9. Fast or Slow?
10. Statics, Walk-Throughs, Jog-Throughs, Run-Throughs
11. Isolation & Stripped-Out Drills
12. Cross Over Sessions
13. General Training For Optimal Results
14. Final Thoughts

Dedication

This is my third book following on from The Fast Bowler's Bible and Coaching Youth Cricket. I want to dedicate this book to the memory of my father, Doug Pont, who passed in 1990 but was a massive inspiration to me in terms of working with junior players.

Whilst I worked with International cricketers my father had the passion for exclusively coaching youth players and won an award for services to sport in 1976, as a coach. He dedicated his coaching life to helping others. It made me understand the importance of keeping things simple and getting to the truth.

I offer this book to every coach, fast bowling wannabe and parent as a way forward.

And to all those who believe you shouldn't prioritise technique, cannot coach speed and avoid working too much on bowling actions – this book is written with you in mind.

It is basic ignorance that has inspired me to pass on the truth about fast bowling coaching.

And to try to be at least as good as my father.

Acknowledgements and Thanks

My special thanks to the following:

Ron Watson (contribution)
John Edge (contribution)
Catherine Dalton (model)
Frocester Cricket Club (venue)
Writtle Indoor Cricket Centre (venue)
Sports Training Advisor.com (contribution)

About The Author, Ian Pont

Ian Pont is regarded as the world's leading fast bowling coach for developing actions and increasing the pace of a bowler. He has worked with world-class international fast bowlers, first-class cricketers, young emerging talent and junior players.

His private cricket coaching, Mavericks Cricket Institute (MCI), is open to all levels of cricketer.

This is Ian's third book following on from The Fast Bowler's Bible in 2006 and Coaching Youth Cricket in 2010.

Ian is a UKCC/ECB Level 3 Head Coach.

He was former ECB National Skills Set Coach for fast bowling and fast bowling coach to both Essex CCC and Northamptonshire CCC and consultant to Ranji Trophy team, Haryana. He has worked with Academy systems, EPP programmes, High Performance Units and helped set up an International Pro Camp in Potchefstroom, South Africa.

Ian is a three-time, ICC World Cup coach having been at the England camp in 2003 in South Africa, in the West Indies with The Netherlands in 2007, and with the host nation Bangladesh at the 2011 World Cup.

Ian was Head Coach of the Dhaka Gladiators in 2012 that won the inaugural BPL T20 competition.

He runs coach education courses and lectures on how to increase both speed & accuracy in fast bowlers.

Mavericks Cricket Institute

All coaching enquiries:
www.maverickscricket.com

Why This Book?

Your Two and a Half Second Coach

It's been frustrating to see the poor standard of fast bowling coaching globally.

Bowlers are often left alone to 'fully develop' according to so-called experts, yet end up with injury-prone actions. And instead of making often quite simple (and certainly obvious) changes those young quicks are grooving incorrect movements and biomechanics that are inefficient.

This means that they have to compensate for problems and never quite fulfil their speed potential or length of career. Worse still, we discover stress injuries of spine, intercostal, knees and ankles as stresses are carried incorrectly through the body.

It does partly explain why we have seen the plethora of Strength & Conditioning coaches in cricket – to help make players 'stronger' (instead of better). Strength and stability have tended to be used as watch words for avoiding teaching correct actions in many cases. Yet the truth is Strength & Conditioning has a vital role to play.

The secrets of coaching pace and accuracy have yet to be picked up by much of the world. The plain truth is that basic knowledge of creating pace bowlers has not been known. Fast bowling is a process and like all processes, it can be learned.

The book allows all coaches, all players and all those involved with cricket at all levels to once and for all understand just how to achieve those ends.

The Fast Bowler's Bible was ground breaking in 2006. This book finishes off what that book started. This one has the drills to go with the interventions and tweaks. If you choose to improve, this book will help you do exactly that.

The reason this book is your two and a half second coach is that it focuses on the most important part of pace bowling – the part that takes around two and half seconds. It starts as you approach the crease, includes your jump to the crease and then your action through it.

Master those two and half seconds and you master speed and accuracy.

I share with you everything I know about pace and accuracy. I hope you enjoy it.

Introduction

We stand on a breakthrough in fast bowling coaching. Whether it is viewed as that remains to be seen. But the truth is, at last, you can discover exactly what you need to do to bowl fast or coach others to bowl fast. This information in its complete form, has never been written down in a book before and the facts about generating speed and accuracy together are backed up with a lifetime's work, plus all the skill drills you need to go with them. The answers are now available to anyone and it's a revolution that you can take part in by learning exactly what you need to do.

So let's get this out there early. You can bowl fast and straight. *The Fast Bowler's Bible* should have shown you that is possible. This book does what *The Fast Bowler's Bible* didn't do – it gives you the drills that go with each of the tweaks that you want to make. However it goes far further than that.

This is a blueprint for pace and accuracy

I wanted to write this book now because having travelled to many Test playing countries and spoken to hundreds of high-level coaches, it is clear that there is no consensus on how to bowl fast - even from them. It would be useful to have some pace bowling guidelines with regarding to coaching, that everyone can use and develop talent. What is evident is that nothing remotely useful is coming from coach educators on this subject and thus the coaches themselves rely on urban myths, wives tales and good old-fashioned incorrect information.

To those of you who have the incorrect belief that fast bowlers are born and not made (which was covered in *The Fast Bowler's Bible*) are doctors born? Are racing drivers born, scientists, surgeons, dentists, architects or any other profession you choose to mention? Clearly we know that fast bowling is a process and since humans are process-based learners, we can learn how to bowl fast.

It doesn't mean that certain people aren't pre-disposed with natural attributes and some people, without the slightest coaching, can fling the cricket ball quickly. In the same way people can run fast, or jump high, hit hard or swim quickly. But It isn't about genetics, height, diet or other factors, as all of the processes for improving performance can be learned. Partly the problem exists because coaches tell people they cannot bowl fast. The only reason you would do this, is if you didn't know how to coach it.

So I want to keep very complex information simple. I want everyone who reads this to be able to understand the processes of pace bowling. And I want everyone to be able to take this information and apply it. After all it is not knowledge that is important but the use of knowledge that will make you a better coach or player.

It therefore comes in two parts to coach speed – understanding how it is generated, then being able to apply it to live bowlers.

What I have done is explain how to bowl fast, then break down the reasons why that particular drill works and how you should go about training yourself to do it 'naturally'. When you have adopted and adapted the new movements into your action then you will feel they have been there all along. This book is a walk-through guide to assist you if you seek ultimate pace.

What I wanted to also do is bust the many, many myths that surround fast bowling coaching. As you go through this book you will discover that there are some things you thought about fast bowling that might be shown to be just plain wrong. It stems from people never really questioning what they hear from others and simply repeating it as fact. Sadly much of it doesn't stand up to scrutiny. So we will show how pace is correctly generated and why the movements create power in your body to accelerate the ball out of your hand.

Strength & Conditioning coaching (S&C) has an important role to play as a function of fast bowling but not *instead* of it

Let me be blunt. You do not bowl faster just because you are stronger. You cannot 'muscle the ball" down to the batsman. Strength helps the body take the strain and rigours of the stresses that apply within the action, but the size of the muscle is not the deciding factor in generating speed in fast bowling.

I say this because teaching a bowler to compensate for problems of injury due to a poor action is not eliminating the cause of any issue.

Understanding how to bowl fast and straight and having all the skill drills and correction techniques to go with it, can feel a little like being someone who knows where all the gold is buried but has no road map. I wanted to chart that road map so others could discover fast bowling 'gold'. So this book is your guide if you choose to follow it. It is a blueprint for producing fast bowlers - or at least those who can maximise what natural attributes they already have.

The one thing you need as a coach is a receptive audience. Plus you need to have full access to players and a large pool of them to have some success with. That is why I hope coaches who are in charge of fast bowling development, at all levels are open-minded to producing 100 mph fast bowlers regularly with the same progress that other sports have made such as running, throwing and swimming. It's almost a 'no-brainer' to develop pace bowlers and we are already way behind in technical terms. Other than simply relying on Strength & Conditioning to make players fitter, the information is out there for improvement in actions that not only help prevent injury but also increase speed and control.

Hats off to anyone who wants to start learning how to produce genuine pace bowlers.

And one final thing before we start. If you stop for a second, that's where you'll finish. What I mean by that is you can do it. You can change your action by applying the drills and knowledge contained in this book. The only person who can stop you – is you.

Your challenge is in filtering the information you will be given based on anecdotal evidence, stories, tips of what others used to do and good old fashioned myths about speed.

Good luck with that and enjoy the journey.

1

Welcome To Russia

We ought to start by taking you through how and why certain body parts help create the overall speed of the ball and where it goes. Throughout this book we will refer to the acronym RSSSA, or Russia. I want you to remember this because it will help your understanding of what is important in delivering ultimate pace and control. What does RSSSA stand for?

R = RANGE of motion
S = SPEED of movement
S = SEQUENCING of muscles
S = SEPARATION of body parts
A = ALIGNMENT of the body position

You will need ALL FIVE components of RSSSA if you are to maximise your speed and accuracy. Before I move off this point, there are very many international fast bowlers who are missing parts of RSSSA. That doesn't make them bad people. It simply means they have developed an action without RSSSA in place in it's entirety and guess what? Had they developed an action with RSSSA they would have no doubt maxmised their fullest potential.

We can never say in sport, particularly when it comes to fast bowling, that any one thing is a definitive. We can only produce 'guidelines' that are a result of benchmarking. But here's the thing. In more than 20 years of working with ABSAT (Advanced Biomechanics Speed and Accuracy Techniques) that my own company MCI, has been utilising, I have seen some *dramatic* and **permanent increases** in both pace and control from bowlers I work with regularly.

There is proof positive that by putting the body into the 'correct' positions shown in this book, that an uplift in skill levels and quality of bowling is possible. What's more, incidences of injuries have been dramatically reduced. I do not have any bowlers who have back injuries or suffer from stress fractures due to the action.

So what is RSSSA? And how does it help you be faster and more accurate?

R = RANGE OF MOTION

The range of motion refers to the distance through which your body moves (and ultimately the ball itself). This is defined by the positions you get into and how flexible your body movements are.

In broad terms, the more distance you travel, the larger the leverage you can create, the more you can 'travel' before letting the ball go, the 'deeper' you can stretch your muscles to create speed and the bigger your arm can finally pull to release the ball. If you are making small movements they may not be as effective as making LARGE ones – providing of course the speed of those movements is quick. There is no point making long, S-L-O-W movements as this will negate the benefits of increasing the range. This brings us onto:

S = SPEED OF MOVEMENT

I have heard some coaches state that 'a short lever is faster than a long one'. This is a very strange statement because if the levers move at the same speed then that's that, plus of course the longer lever gives you more force, as you may recall from your basic physics at school. So now we have established (as in the Range Of Motion) above, that the distance through which we move is a desirable thing to focus on, it is the speed of movement that affects the pace you bowl.

When you make movements faster, you also create a chain of events in the body that happens faster, too. And we all know that the faster the arm comes over the faster the ball comes out. Therefore we seek those movements in the body to happen quickly but clearly, in sequence.

S = SEQUENCING OF MUSCLES

The body delivers the ball with a complex series of muscle stretches and contractions. Effectively, the muscles are 'elastic' and like a bow and arrow you are attempting to get the body in a chain reaction of stretching and contracting.

This sequence creates a 'ripple effect' through the body and this is the feeling of rhythm or timing that a bowler sometimes feels. When you get the sequencing right it feels great. Get it wrong and it feels like you have your feet in concrete.

It explains why some bowlers try to bowl 'with their shoulder' because the top half happens last and if all else fails, they just want to hurl the ball down the other end. We are looking to be smarter than that. And in this book you will find out that the LAST thing you do is bowl the cricket ball – literally. Everything else moves before that happens.

S = SEPARATION OF BODY PARTS

I am not talking about being a serial killer here. Separation of body parts means that the body acts like a five stage rocket. And like a five stage rocket the energy in transferred to each section above, making that movement faster.

A bowler bowls first with their legs, then their hips, then their chest, then their shoulders and finally their arm. The wrist also plays a role with the control of the ball and it's release, but it is the five stages before this that take the energy up the body, accelerating the movement into the back of the ball. It is this series that dictates how coordinated you are and how effective you are at using all your body to bowl the ball.

We will refer to RSSSA through this book. If you are unsure what each part means at that time you can easily refer to the simple explanations above for clarity.

The idea is to make this as easy to follow as possible and not to complicate matters. I have heard coaches talk about 'eco-centric load ups', 'clear pathways' and 'energy leaks' when referring to bowling actions with coaches and players. But we want to lose this gobbledegook language and redefine the terminology that makes understanding simpler, effective and more importantly, something a player can actually go and put into practice.

A = ALIGNMENT OF THE BODY POSITION

If you run up straight, go through the crease straight and follow through straight, there's a very high chance the ball will go straight. In addition, we know that the shortest distance between two points is a straight line. This covers accuracy and speed TOGETHER. But alignment isn't just about straight lines. It is also about putting your body into the right positions to maximise what you have naturally.

So it should come as no surprise to learn that within the action itself, including all the small movements as well as the big ones, movements affect the success of a bowler. If you are going to make important stretches and contractions as well as maintain an efficient human movement, then things like correct shoulders, hips, feet, legs, chest, head and wrist alignment are hugely vital.

Keep an open mind to how you can become far better positioned in your action, jump and run up to ensure you have a flow of power and energy going through the back of the ball on release.

Coaching is not proving how smart a coach is, but how easy fast bowling improvements are. This is why RSSSA will set you on the road to having a base understanding of what works in the bowling action and potentially what should be worked on.

Let me also say here that all the components of RSSSA are dependent upon each other to be maximised. That is to say that they are far more effective as a team than as individual components. Each part of RSSSA impacts positively on the whole meaning that by tweaking or adjusting just ONE part of RSSSA can lead to improvements in other areas.

That's why learning and understanding what RSSSA is can be a vitally important part of fast bowling development. It is a framework that can be adhered to so that consistency and success become a natural part of someone's evolution as a pace bowler.

2
Small Keys Open Big Locks

Even the smallest change can have a big impact. When you work on tweaking something or changing it, how long should it take?

We have probably all heard the boffins in white coats with big foreheads say it takes 10,000 repetitions to make a change. The change to which they refer is 'muscle memory' or the body's ability to do something without you giving it much thought. But I don't subscribe to that number or repetitions needed.

When I worked with Darren Gough for example, he made a change to his front arm position in his hang time (or jump gather as some refer to it as) that took literally one ball. He tried it and decided that was an improvement he wanted to keep. The change I believe, helped him to be more efficient and thus have an extended career of four further seasons, culminating with a return to Yorkshire CCC as captain.

For Goughie, the small change opened a big door. Plus he bowled as well as he had done since he was a young player coming into the England side.

Does the fact that Darren Gough made this change in one delivery, prove that 10,000 repetitions is wrong to make changes? No, it simply shows that everyone is different, and we don't all subscribe to the same 'generic' stereotypes where the scientific community wants to put people into compartments. This is partly the issue with 'proving' a theory. Unless you can show time after time it is repeatable, it may not be seen 'as fact'.

So I want you to think of this another way. We are humans and humans are fallible. Some like to learn by listening. Some like to learn by watching. Some like to learn by trying it. The truth is most of us are combinations of all three. And this means we will absorb information in different ways and at different speeds. In addition, you will remember much faster and deeper if you consciously think about what you are doing and why you are doing it. When you add emotion to a thought, it becomes burned in your mind and it's something you find hard to forget. The Four Tent Pegs, later on in this book, deals with this in far more detail.

Why am I saying all this?

Because expectation levels of how fast you can learn new things and how quickly you can embed changes into an action change vary from player to player. So don't look at someone else and think you are not as smart as them if they get things faster than you. You will work this at your own pace and you will find parts far easier to grasp than others.

How long should you expect to wait to see changes?

Again, every one of us is completely different. All I can say is that you will need to work through any alterations you make and know that they happen slowly. It will be like watering a plant. That plant may take a number of weeks to even show it is growing. Keep watering the plant. Your changes will be similar to that in most cases. Don't worry. Keep working through your drills. They will look after you.

3

Your Journey To Work

Ok. Let's start off the whole concept of how to bowl fast and straight by discussing the run-up, which is effectively, your journey to work.

The length of your run up, it's speed, intent and also the angle you come in at, is very much a personal issue. What IS important is that your take off stride (jump into your action if you need one – more on that in the next chapter) and the exit stride (immediate follow through stride after you have let the ball go), is straight. Let me be clear by what I mean by straight. I mean that you should be moving in the same direction as the ball. If you are attempting to bowl 'into the channel' or at off stump, then we are trying to ensure that is exactly where we are running.

You may have learned from The Fast Bowler's Bible that if you run up straight, go through the crease straight and follow through straight, that the ball tends to go... straight. If you retain this premise, then as long as you are hitting the crease moving at your target then all of your energy is going to be transported into the action, or at least it will make you as efficient as possible.

Make sure you are running down your own railway track towards the top of the batsman's off stump

I have heard some other International coaches use the word "aggression" when it comes to bowling. Usually, this is encouraged to start with the run up and speed of it. But rather than use the word "aggression", I would rather you thought of the phrase "positive intent". The reason is, that being aggressive doesn't always imply being controlled. We definitely want you to be controlled in what you do. So if you choose a fast approach then ensure it is controlled so you do not hit the crease like a plane coming in far too quickly to land.

Equally, a slow approach can also mean you then have to overuse the top half of your body to try to generate the pace you wish, and you could ultimately lose the shape of your action, plus create unnecessary stresses on shoulders, joints and even your back. The incidences of back injuries appear to be the same, not decreasing despite intervention and bowling restrictions.

So the run up should be fast enough for you to jump into your action by taking off with a feeling of JUMPING IN to the action. You are not trying to do high jump, but rather long jump if you want to get a feeling of momentum. And here's really the key phrase for a run-up.

Momentum is something you should be taking in to your action from your approach. You do not want to lean back when you run in. You are driving your arms backwards and forwards, rather than side to side. You should be running with the left foot landing under the left hip and right foot under right hip. Some people run by 'crossing over' their feet and this causes a misalignment as well as an issue when taking off to bowl. So try to ensure you are moving down a railway track with each foot so it lands under the correct side of your body.

When attacking the left hand batsman's off stump, start your run up a little wider and run at it in a straight line

With regard to different styles of bowling, it ought to be known that a front on bowler (landing with back foot pointing straight down the pitch), will gain greater overall pace of delivery when running in faster. The more sideways the bowler (back foot landing parallel with the bowling crease), the less important the ground speed compared to a front on bowler. Why? Because in the bowling action, the HIPS become vitally important for generating speed. A front on bowler has less hip rotation than a sideways bowler, so a sideways bowler will be able to generate greater speed by this hip rotation.

We will discuss hip rotation in far greater detail further into the book because it will explain in part, exactly why certain bowlers bowl at 85 mph and others at 75 mph.

And just a word here about bowling to a left or right hand batsman. If you accept the idea that you should be running straight at the target (presumably towards the top of off stump) then you will notice the slightly different line up for a right hand bowler to a left hand batsman and vice versa. You can achieve this simply by taking a step out at the end of your run up – to your left if you are a right handed bowler – so that the angle you run from and to, is slightly changed.

If you are confused by angles just remember this: run directly at the target you are trying to hit where possible. Take a point from the end of your run up to that target and run along that line.

We seek the 'A' of RSSSA, which is Alignment.

Whilst run ups are important, they do not account for the largest part of your bowling speed. However, what they ARE important for is in getting you into the right position to bowl effectively, with the right amount of ground speed to launch an efficient and explosive action that generates high body speed.

4

Jump To It

The take off into your bowling action is an important phase of bowling. Because it is this 'leap of faith' that sets your bowling action ready for you to bowl. But it is only a 'phase' or a transition from run up to action – nothing more.

Before we get into the technicalities of it too much, it is quite simple. If you jump into your action in a balanced way, you will be doing yourself a great many favours. If you jump up too high all your momentum will be going up and down. If you jump to the off or to the leg side, then this is how you will be setting your base to bowl and making it far harder to maximise your speed and alignment.

So what is the *ideal* jump into your action?

Make sure you are running down your own railway track towards the top of the batsman's off stump

Well contrary to public coaching opinion, a jump at the crease isn't strictly necessary at all. The closest power movement we have to fast bowling is javelin throwing as we know. Javelin throwers use a simple 'hop' to transfer from the run-up phase into the throwing phase. This 'bound' or jump is very small.

Why their jump is small is that technically, you slow down the longer you are in the air. The higher you jump, the longer you spend in the air. So it is important to understand why a jump at the crease might be desirable for a fast bowler.

I have heard some well-known international coaches say that the jump into the crease is the MOST important thing of all. However, if you understood how pace is generated, how energy is transferred and how the body works to create an explosive force, why would people say this about the jump into the action?

What's clear is coaches are not sure why a jump is biomechanically important. But due to the fact that all bowlers are taught to jump then it's something a coach can focus on without having to work on the bowling action itself perhaps. After all, how hard can a jump be to understand?

For those of you choosing to 'gather' yourself by 'bounding' then you will experience some time in the air. There is a feel factor at work here, in the sense that a jump can help you 'set' your action.

The gauge of a good attack into your action is a great knee drive like this. With a neutral top half, the leading leg powers you up

The technical way to jump therefore is to create a momentary 'hang time' where you jump through the movement. You will experience a slight floating effect and this is where you then set your action. Many bowlers can rush their action if they do not jump, or at least feel as though they are being rushed.

There is a play off here between what feels right, what seems to be controlled and balanced, smooth and rhythmical, compared to what is the most efficient biomechanically to create pace. It is, as always, a 'style versus substance' thing for bowlers where looking good can count as much as being effective. The facts are that this book is called Ultimate Pace Secrets for a reason. And that means you will find all the most effective techniques to develop your pace. Having a large or small leap at the crease depends on what you are trying to achieve.

A good 'neutral' top half is desirable here. Not leaning backwards or forwards in the jump, just a drive to target with legs

For me, it is simply to turn you slightly side on (if that is your style of bowling) – no more than that. In other words, your transition between run up and action ought to be as efficient as possible. It has to suit the way YOU bowl. That means you have to feel it is workable. There is little point scuttling through the crease from a non-existent jump, if you cannot build that into allowing your body to cope with it. You will hit the crease faster and this affects your biomechanics.

If we were building an action from scratch, we would encourage a low drive to the target rather than a large leap, if at all.

You are looking for good 'hang time' where the top half 'sets' and the legs take you through into your landing position

A note here on javelin. The javelin weighs 800 grams and is already set back behind the thrower into the crossover steps. A cricket ball is 154 grams and is carried in front of the bowler. So you may decide you need time to set the ball back behind you when you land on the back foot. If you recall Jeff Thomson from the 1970's, this Australian great fast bowler, and probably one of the fastest of all time, had a javelin style move where he crossed his feet over and left his bowling arm way back behind him into the crease.

This crossover move undoubtedly set him up for the pace he created and developed a huge range of motion (R) that fired the ball out at speeds around 100 mph (160 kph) on a regular basis.

So my message to you here is if you are going to jump, make sure you are balanced, moving towards the target and not leaping too high for your style of bowling.

5

Technique Is Not The Most Important Thing. It's The ONLY Thing

One of the greatest thrills watching the London 2012 Olympics, apart from watching athletes at the peak of their careers, was discovering how they became the champions they are.

When listening to interviews with coaches, athletes, former champions and commentators, the *overwhelming* **common denominator of their success** was getting the **technical aspect** of their sport right.

Whether rowing a boat, cycling on the track or running a race, the deciding factor seemed to be HOW they rowed, cycled or ran that made the most difference. People constantly spoke about the technique of the athlete and how small tweaks often made the biggest uplift in performance.

It brings me to the one thing that has always bothered me about cricket coaching. It's the fact that when it comes to coaching batting, coaches spend 99% of their time teaching the technical aspects, yet on bowling coaching they spend none – almost literally.

A coach in a net or session with a player will talk about "balance, head position, body weight, alignment, foot positioning, shape of shots, moving feet, high elbows, etc., etc.," as well as probably review video clips showing their technical flaws and what's needed to correct them.

When it comes to fast bowling there is virtually none. And what miniscule amount of coaching technically there is doesn't have much relevance to actually generating more speed. What the coaches all focus on instead is how the ball is held, the wrist position and hitting the top of off stump. This is the athletics equivalent of telling a sprinter to run fast in a straight line towards the finish.

Fast bowling seems to be treated as an 'outcome-based' coaching session and batting a 'process-based' coaching session. Yet humans are process-based learners. If you coached batting like coaches coach bowling then all you would say to a batsman is' "Hold the bat like this and hit it through there". Interesting.

The truth is we all know exactly why fast bowling coaching is like it is. And let's face it. The quality of understanding on fast bowling coaching is probably the worst in any major sport. To have such little knowledge on a highly specialised subject can only be gotten away with, if no one really understands it, including those who coach the coaches. This is exactly what we have. And also explains why, to comfort themselves, a coach will most likely say, "fast bowlers are born". So this further makes it less likely to want to find out how and why speed & accuracy are created. I have even had conversations with coaches who have said to me, "speed cannot be taught". Worse still, those coaches then mistakenly think that building muscles and strength in the gym alone is somehow going to create pace bowlers.

This is where the game of cricket has come to right now.

I speak to hundreds and hundreds of parents of young players involved with teams at all levels and they say they cannot even find a bowling coach, let alone many who know about pace. This is because the coaches themselves know very little about coaching pace into bowlers, yet they know a huge amount about how to coach pace OUT of them. "Slow down, bowl a line and length" is what most say. "Get your arm as high as possible and brush your ear" is another. "Stand up and bowl tall because you will get more bounce", is the final one.

I will help you in this book dispel those myths and explain why

So if the coaches don't know how to coach speed presumably it's because they have never been taught how to coach it. And those teaching the coaches therefore don't know either. If you are a player or parent reading this book you will now start to realise why fast bowling coaching is where it is and why there are virtually no pace coaches around to help.

The correct information isn't there to be taught or learned. It's the one area of the game that seems to mystify an entire cricket community. What is around are injury prevention directives and complex biomechanical information on being safe in the bowling action. This is an important factor, but what's missed is that it can be achieved by being efficient in the action, instead of piling on restrictions. Why stop people bowling rather than getting them to be better in the first place? And subsequently we see a massive rise in strength & conditioning (S&C), with every team seemingly having a coach for fitness as the answer. As I said in the introduction, S&C is important, but only as a function of fast bowling, not as a replacement for it skill wise or technically.

At this time of writing, I have heard that some youth representative sides are now being selected on fitness rather than skill. I seriously had to ask the parents who told me this to repeat that, as I couldn't believe what I was hearing. This sadly will mean even LESS work being done on skills (as the time is being used up jumping through rope ladders or hopping over small hurdles and jumping on mini trampolines for 'core stability'). So the speed, skill and technical part of fast bowling continues to be completely overlooked.

When you start from a place of lack and restriction, and only look at a narrow field, you miss how to develop the bowling action to overcome those issues anyway.

A correct action technically gives you less stresses, strains and chances of being injured, plus of course it makes you faster and more accurate

When I started coaching I was desperate to try and simplify the overuse of technical jargon that some bowling coaches were starting to use. It led me to researching 1000's of bowling actions over a long period of time and look at common traits that led to certain bowlers bowling fast whilst others bowled military medium.

I looked into my past as a baseball pitcher and looked at how power is generated there. But the closest movement to pace bowling is a javelin throw and during the past decade, I have been fortunate to work with some world experts in the power generation systems in the body, required to project an object as far – and thus as fast – as possible.

The work I had done started to galvanise my thoughts in new areas and away from traditional fast bowling coaching of "standing tall" and also "brushing your ear" when bowling. I began to work on a completely different level with new ideas and concepts. Plus, the hardest part of all, I had to come up with skill drills to go with those exciting discoveries about speed.

The point is it is no good being able to understand how to generate pace if you cannot teach others how to do it themselves

What's more, everyone's action is unique so we cannot exactly create a definitive here for pace bowling.

What we can do though is produce guidelines. And these guidelines offer any bowler the framework for maximizing speed and accuracy. Those guidelines are known as The Four Tent Pegs, which we detail later.

They came about from wishing to give my students the simplest ideas and positions they could apply to their own actions, to make themselves as efficient as possible. They had to be robust, repeatable, easy to learn but more than all this, provable they would increase speed. The huge number of testimonials to speed increases and improvements in accuracy are proof positive that we have indeed found the key to speed & accuracy. For whilst RSSSA explains to us WHY the body generates the speed it does, The Four Tent Pegs shows us HOW it's done. The great news is anyone can use them and anyone can learn them to become better fast bowlers.

As I said above though, these are guidelines only. That's because for every Brett Lee action that's full of wonderful, natural movements, there's a Shaun Tait action of simply raw power. For each Sohail Tanvir and Lasith Malinga, there's an Allan Donald. In other words, just because bowlers might not get into the four tent pegs positions perfectly, doesn't make them poor bowlers. Bowlers evolve with an action unchecked and learn to adapt to it. This becomes their 'natural' bowling action. But what exactly IS natural?

If you do something enough times it becomes natural

So if you were to learn the 'correct' way to increase your speed and trained that, then this would become your 'natural' action.

That's the great thing about humans and process-based learning - we all have the capability to learn in our heads. If you can view fast bowling techniques as a process, then you can learn it. The Four Tent Pegs highlight the four key positions in the crease that you should try to get into when you bowl. The drills that go with those positions help you learn the process to cement into your own action.

As we go through this process and the positions in turn, they will also pop up many questions for us to answer. Some of this will lead to a complete overhaul of current MIS-thinking about fast bowling and make much of what is being taught by coaches and people who coach them, as redundant.

You must remember that through this book we are interested in being as fast and as accurate as possible. The positive side-effects of utilising the drills is you will be grooving a safe action, that is repeatable, powerful and give you huge consistency.

It is the reason this book was written in the first place.

Why the tent peg positions are massively important though, is due to another factor about how you should learn or teach, technical information. And that is we learn far more easily when we break down the vital movements into smaller, bite-sized pieces. This is known as 'chunking' or practicing small 'chunks' of the bowling action so they can be mastered.

In truth, the fast bowling action isn't one continuous movement. It is in fact a highly complex and complicated series of small moves, or chunks, that are performed one after another. It is only by identifying what these chunks are, that you can then start to work on improving them.

The Four Tent Pegs are those chunks. They are the chunks of the bowling action that lead to both speed and accuracy. They are the chunks that when performed correctly, enable the body to be at it's most efficient. And this means as stress-free as possible due to being as efficient as possible.

It means being repeatable. Above all, it means being consistent

You will not be able to make highly complex moves without first looking at the action you want to have in its entirety and then going out and 'drilling' those individual parts that make up the action.

So how you do this, is to practice the Four Tent Pegs individually and then when you have mastered each one, put the parts together. You will also have to do the drills as low speeds to get the exact movements. You need to be able to feel each position. Look in a mirror when you are doing them if you can or review a video clip of yourself.

You will not need a cricket ball. The last thing you want is to hold a ball and run up to bowl. You are trying to 'overwrite' an action to be able to change it. So repeating what you do normally will simply revert back to what is natural for you. This explains why coaches are rarely successful trying to make changes to bowlers in the nets.

Instead, slow everything down, walk it through, make the moves from static positions – even do what I refer to as a MEGA drill.

This is where you go the other way with your speed and attempt to perform the action chunks in SUPER SLOW MOTION. This is incredibly hard to do and it also isn't very comfortable. That's a good thing. You want to be able to learn how the muscles work and how it feels to be in those new positions. If you cannot do the movements slowly, you will not do them fast. It is as this point we are working with SEQUENCING and understanding what parts of the body works when.

You are trying to create precision when you do your drills. Pay attention to detail. Don't allow misalignments. If you start off with a poor foot position in a drill you will start to engrain it. Make sure that everything you do is world-class. When you do this then you give yourself the best chance of improving faster.

If you can get a sense of the mistakes you are making in drills then the improvements can come faster. You should welcome difficulty and awkwardness as a sign of change. Things are happening. If they feel easy then you are cruising along and no one ever learns anything when they just cruise. So try to make your practices and drills as intense and meaningful as possible. Don't do them half-heartedly. Do them with a passion to get them right. Each time you make a mistake it's a step closer to them being better.

Let's discuss The Four Tent Pegs now and the positions you should get extra friendly with.

6

The Four Tent Pegs
Dare, Fail, Learn, Adapt, Succeed, Repeat

I want to give you an unfettered overview of the guideline positions you ought to strive to achieve in your action. After this we will go into exactly how to drill each one, the common mistakes bowlers make and the difficulties and challenges with making corrections.

Before I do that though, here's something you can ask any bowler to do so you can see where they naturally strive to get their pace from. In a session, ask the bowler to bowl as fast as possible. Really crank it up and bowl the fastest ball they are capable of. Say to them not to care where it goes either.

What you are looking for is the length they bowl. This will tell you whether they use their bottom half or top half to bowl.

If the top half is too active, too reliant on for generating pace then the bowler will bowl short. This is because the release point changes to deliver the ball 'later' and the bowler will not know why. All they are doing is releasing the ball with the same timing of a normal paced delivery but of course the extra top half speed means that release point is further advanced – hence a short ball. They simply hang onto the ball too long. So the feet and hips have to 'catch up' to bowl a length and thus effectively bowl even faster.

If the legs or base is too active (fast feet for example) then the bowler will tend to bowl a full toss, maybe even a beamer. This is because the release point is now too early for the timing of the bowler as the ground speed is higher. The top half has to 'catch up' to bowl a length and thus bowl even faster.

A bowler bowling uphill or downhill temporarily feels this phenomenon. Some bowlers cannot bowl down a slope. Others can only bowl up it and vice versa.

Why it is useful to know this as a coach or player, is that to alter the speed a bowler bowls at, takes an understanding of what body parts move and when they move. The timing and coordination of the movements is precise and happens in microseconds. It explains why a bowler running in too fast or too slow can also feel a complete lack of rhythm. And it also explains why we need at least a framework to hang the action on in the first place.

Welcome to the Four Tent Pegs.

TENT PEG ONE

The first tent peg is when you make your first commitment to actually bowl. This happens as soon as your back foot hits the ground in your action. You have started to think about bowling the ball at this point and you have set your action ready to be unfolded in the correct sequence.

Your back foot impact position is all your own. By that I mean you should land it where it feels most comfortable and you will then take your line up based on where it points. This dictates what type of bowler you are: front on, midway/semi, or sideways. These are the three main landing positions that the vast majority of bowlers get into, or points in between.

Please look at the images opposite to see which one you are.

In rough terms, a front on bowler's back foot will point straight down the pitch, a midway bowler's back foot will point at around 45 degrees and the sideways bowler will have a parallel to the crease position, or 90 degrees to front on.

None is better than any other, except for one thing. And that thing is Range of Motion. If you are sideways you can move your hips through a fuller range of motion than a front on bowler. This has an impact on speed because as we will discover, an increase of hip speed (range of motion) creates an increase of bowling shoulder speed and ultimately ball speed – if you have the correct sequencing.

In crude terms, and without complicating the issue, a sideways bowler pound for pound will be faster than a front on bowler for pretty much this fact alone. That is of course assuming a sideways bowler actually uses the hips correctly and doesn't waste it, which is a whole other issue. This is why ground speed for a front on bowler is more important, as they cannot get as much hip turn so have to increase hip speed from base speed levels (run up and speed through the crease).

The tent pegs will show how to fully utilise the hips and other positions in the bowling action regardless of your current back foot impact position.

Tent Peg One for a sideways bowler

Tent Peg One for a semi or midway bowler

Tent Peg One for a front on bowler

I want to just take a slight side road at this time because I have seen some coaches teaching "hopping" on the back foot over plastic cones on the floor or over small yellow hurdles. I have even seen coaches getting bowlers to jump from a bench onto their back leg. Many will know exactly what I am referring to.

This is not a very good drill for pace bowling and I will tell you why

The LAST thing you want to teach your body to do is stop on back foot impact in the bowling action. The back foot impact is a 'moving' position where your core strength and stability help you lift your front leg and drive it down so you can bowl.

If you consider this for a moment you will realise that 'teaching' your proprioception (the body's ability to sense movement within joints and joint position) to stop on the back foot in this way simply makes the transfer of energy from your run up even harder. Worse still, to balance, many people lean back in this position to try to keep their balance instead of moving forward into the front foot block.

I first saw this drill in the mid-2000's as the so-called answer to balancing and training the body for core stability. But what those in coaching have failed to understand is that by isolating the movement in this way, you are teaching yourself to be static and not learning about the movement through a RANGE of motion.

There are *better exercises* for training core stability that do not emulate the fast bowling action (if that's what this drill is meant to be about). Therefore you avoid the coaching skills trap of learning a bad habit, which is what can happen when you do it 'in context' (next to stumps or holding a ball in your hand).

So please understand you want to replicate what the bowling action actually does in context and not training something that is a strength & conditioning issue disguised as a bowling drill. Isolation drills are great provided you learn them as part of a sequence.

The key for ensuring you are lined up correctly with your hips and shoulders is to imagine there is a piece of string hanging down and linking your front knee and your front elbow together, rather like a puppet string. This means that the elbow and the knee will be lined up in the same plane, and thus your hips and shoulders.

The idea is to raise the front knee up to around waist level thus engaging the glute muscles and the hip flexors to assist with generating some power into the front foot impact that happens in tent peg 2.

In fact this line up is a 3 second fix for bowlers who have a mixed action (where the hips and shoulders are misaligned). By simply ensuring the front elbow and front knee are lined up underneath one another, you ensure your hips and shoulders are too.

You should remember that it is always far harder to change the base of your action than the top. Once your base is built, very much like the foundations of a house, they are hard to dig up and reset. So if you have to make any adjustments to alignment, try to make them based on the bottom half of your action if you can. It is not impossible to alter the base work of any action, let's be clear. And in many cases you will have to simply alter something at the base. It is just far harder to do that.

I want to mention something here about the back foot contact

Should you wish to make the most of the back foot contact position with regard to bowling fast, then you do not want to be landing very hard into this position. What I mean by that is a jolting, harsh impact at this point will ultimately stop much of your momentum. It isn't on *back foot contact* that we seek to stop bowling. The momentum must continue to drive the bottom half through the action. This explains why practicing the hopping exercise (as mentioned earlier) really does us no favours whatsoever and in fact teaches the wrong 'feeling' for the bowling action on back foot contact.

Instead, I want you to think of your back foot as being a 'light touch'. Now clearly all your body weight is going through this position and when you are landing from your take off, you are going to be bringing all of that into your back foot contact. But think of your weight registering 'zero' on a set of weighing scales. Imagine that feeling for a moment if you will. You 'touch down' in your back foot contact but it isn't a heavy Jumbo Jet style landing. To achieve this you will probably want to land on the ball of your back foot ready to move into the delivery stride itself fairly quickly. Keep it light, keep it fast.

Remember, we do not wish to do anything that will take away ground speed and transfer of energy into the front foot impact, which happens in tent peg 2.

At the moment we practice holding the key position of tent peg 1, we will clearly be supporting our body weight on the back foot contact position and this is of course necessary to establish how it looks (alignment). This position is just a frame or two on a camera because we are moving THROUGH this position into the next one. When you take snap shots like the 4 tent pegs, they merely serve as checkpoints for your bowling action and not designed to be static in themselves.

MOST COMMON MISTAKES

Not being 'neutral' with top half body weight

When the back foot impacts it is ideal to have the top half not leaning forwards or too far backwards. The legs have to do their job first so you should ideally maintain a non-committed top half at this point. The phrase 'bend your back' is a bad one as it creates a thought of leaning away from the direction of movement. You also want to 'sink' into your second tent peg and the top half position remains neutral to make that possible.

Landing too hard on the back foot (stopping momentum)

The LAST thing you want to do is land hard on your back foot and lose all your momentum. This is a huge mistake because your run up speed is stopped before you bowl. Landing hard or stiff legged reduces your speed and means you are likely to push your top half too far ahead of using the legs instead of creating a 'ground upwards' domino effect.

Misalignment (mix)

Apart from having issues with your back, the mixed action where your top half misaligns with your bottom half, can make your release point harder to be consistent, as well as reduce your speed. If you seek efficiency then you will seek perfect alignment going into your front foot block – rather than make it more difficult to do so.

You can see from the image that the ball is also set off from underneath the wrong armpit, and this will mean the bowling hand will go back towards the umpire when the bowler pulls their arm back, instead of in a straight line towards the sight screen.

TENT PEG TWO

This is the front foot impact position. It is effectively half way through the bowling action and is the position from where you generate your pace and accuracy.

Tent Peg Two

In basic terms, if you think of the body as a 5-point star (head, both feet and both hands) at this time then you will have it right. This is also the biggest STRETCH in the body and your hands ought to be as far away from one another as possible on opposite sides.

To get the timing of this you will note that as your front foot lands your front hand will 'grab at the batsman's collar'. Most fast bowlers 'lose' their front arm at this time and the hand is down by their side. But this is incorrect timing because you require a stable base (front foot impact) to have something to pull against. If your front arm drops down before your front foot impact then you have pulled it against fresh air instead of a solid position. It is hard to estimate just how much lost speed happens if you lose the front arm but if we conservatively said 5-8 mph then you can see just how important it is.

We will come on to the front arm pull in tent peg 3 but from a range of motion, sequencing and alignment viewpoint, getting the front arm s-t-r-e-t-c-h-e-d out to target on impact is highly desirable.

The bowling hand at the same time, should be pointing directly back to the sightscreen. In a dead straight line behind you. This will give you the longest stretch through the back of the ball when you bowl. It will also help you line up to the target correctly for accuracy as well as maximise your length of lever.

So many bowlers do not come straight back to the sightscreen as they pull their arm back into tent peg 2 and so misalign the upswing of their bowling arm. This means they can bowl "in to out" and push the ball from the wrong side of their body when they release the ball in tent peg 3.

The bottom half of the body must also align correctly, too. The front foot should line up so it supports the front bowling shoulder. The landing of this foot ought to be in line with your front hip directly aiming at the batsman's off stump. To help you further with this line-up, if you were to slide your foot back underneath your body so you are standing normally, it will be directly under your hip as would happen when you are standing normally.

I have to comment on what I have heard as landing your feet in a straight line (as if you are on a tightrope) and this is called landing in the corridor. Please do not do this. If you have ever tried to stand with your feet in a dead straight line (as on a tightrope) you will know how unbalanced this is. Your front foot impact MUST support your non-bowling side so when you pull against it, it is stable and your front hip can lock. You will see why in Tent Peg 3.

This front foot landing is known as the 'plant' into the ground or 'block' and is your second commitment to bowl. Once that foot is planted into the ground you cannot move it. So you will want to ensure it is as **strong and as stable as possible**. Up to six times your body weight can go through the front leg when bowling so this plant is vital to establishing the platform to drive hard against and be as efficient as possible in transferring energy towards the batsman.

Sadly, I see very many fast bowlers 'shutting off' their feet by planting the front foot a little across their body so it is going towards the leg side as they bowl. This means they will have to bowl AROUND their front leg and most likely, not be using it correctly as a stable column to pull against. Additionally, many bowlers who bowl this way also collapse their front leg and thus lose a huge amount of ground speed momentum. We will cover this more fully in tent peg 3 but if the front leg 'eases off' by bending, or worse still dramatically collapses then the power of the hips can also be lost.

MOST COMMON MISTAKES

Bending the front leg

The bending of the front knee is the most common mistake as it is hard to straighten the front leg, once it has landed bent. This knee may have bent on impact and it is that loss of the braking force in the front leg that leaks all the energy away, instead of using the reactional force of your leg impacting the turf and staying locked.

Not being fully stretched

If you are not grabbing the sightscreen from behind and the batsman's collar from the front, then you are not fully stretched. Imagine an elastic band and you will appreciate how vital that stretch is in making a powerful release. The bigger the stretch, the more range of motion you get, and stretch reflex. By shortening your arms you do not maximise your speed and are likely to release the ball as a 'flick' rather than a powerful pull.

Crossing The Feet Over

Ideally, we seek the front foot supporting the front knee, hip and shoulder in a column. Here we see that with the foot crossed over, the energy is 'shut off' and the bowler cannot fully use their hips.

This position can lead to knee issues too, with a twisting or rotational force going through the joints and ligaments. In addition, a bowler can have back issues over time. With the feet going one way and the top half the other, a misalignment of energy and pull through is created.

Throwing the front arm away

This is a true sign the top half of the action is ahead in timing of the bottom half and the bowling and non-bowling sides of the action do not work with each other. The position is often created because a bowler throws both hands forward in the action in tent peg 1. On heel strike, the front arm is ready to be pulled but by throwing away the front arm too early a bowler can lose up to 5-8 mph.

Not having top half 'neutral'

When the front foot impacts the top half should not lean forwards. The reason is that the legs 'go first' by transferring the ground speed into the top half through the hips. If the top half is already engaged when the front foot hits, it means the hip power and core speed cannot be used sequentially. The bottom half is followed by the top half – not the other way round.

Head falling to off side - Lateral Flexion

Many things can cause lateral flexion – a high bowling hip, no drop step, misaligned feet or just a good old-fashioned head fall. The result might not only be an ugly action but one that could lead to back issues. Intercostal injuries as well as stress fractures are common complaints when the spine has lateral flexion. In addition, speeds drop and the release point is badly affected. The ball is thus being 'pushed' in towards the batsman generally.

7

Drop Step, Front Foot Block, Stretch Reflex

I'm giving this a whole chapter to itself. That's because I feel the Drop Step, Front Foot Block and Stretch Reflex, really identify what pace bowling coaching should all be about.

Technically speaking, the drop step happens when you move from tent peg 1 into tent peg 2. The front foot block is where your front leg lands straight and stays straight, so you can bowl AGAINST it, not over it. This is why it's called a block.

As a fast bowler, your power should come from your legs and specifically your hips. The 'drop step, front-foot block' movement is a power/speed generator that Javelin throwers use. This is a technique that fast bowlers can learn from.

DROP STEP

What is it?

A 'drop step, front foot block' is simpler than maybe it sounds. It means that in your bowling stride, your front leg is straight, while your back leg is bent as you drag your back foot through the crease and bowl. You drag the back foot to keep your hip flexors fully engaged and the power switched on.

You're also trying to create a shoulder-hip separation. This is where your shoulders and your hips are some way apart from each other. Reaching that position, with your arm out behind you, you create a 'stretch reflex' where your arm will be propelled forwards as your body naturally, instinctively moves your shoulders back to facing forwards, in alignment with your hips. That stretch reflex movement creates power from the core of the body.

A new way of thinking

This technique isn't what most cricket coaches will tell you: they'll tell you not to bend your back leg at any cost. They believe you shouldn't 'collapse' your back leg in your bowling stride because you'll end up delivering the ball from a lower position.

But the simple fact is that everybody collapses their back leg to a greater or lesser degree, as they drive through the crease. Rather than trying to coach fast bowlers to avoid doing it, I want to make them aware that, in fact, this is where a lot of their speed can come from.

The idea that a snapshot of a bowler at point of delivery will show the body standing straight and tall like a column, the ball 12 inches above the bowler's full height is simply wrong.

Land 'soft' on the ball of the back foot. slightly flexing the back leg

You can use a door frame, or any fixed point to practice keeping your arm back and turning your hips forward. This shoulder/hip separation drill helps you understand how the hips engage first and the shoulder and arm drive second

At point of delivery, the body shape is more or less a 'V'shape: the legs and the top body make a right angle.

The back foot should be pointing forward as the knee 'drops' into the block (hence the name drop step). The hips and body will 'sink' into the front foot impact

When Brett Lee's front foot lands, his hips are set back at about 45 degrees from his foot. His top half is thrown forward, 45 degrees from his hips, creating a 'V' shape. Lee's head is probably at chest-height to the non-striking batsman. Lee is around 6'1" but when he delivers the ball his head is at around 5'4". This comes from having a large drop step, or bend from the back knee.

Your back leg will come through bent anyway. What I want to do is show you why consciously working on bending your back leg in the right way will make you a faster.

Why it works

Imagine running across the road and tripping over the kerb. When you hit the kerb, your foot stops and your top half is thrown forward. And the same principle applies in fast bowling but in a more controlled way.

Once you "block' your front foot, by creating a solid base as an anchor to your action, the top half of your body and ultimately your bowling arm shoot forward.

The front leg locks out or 'blocks' and rapidly decelerates all the forward ground speed. This transfers into the top half. Back foot will start to drag from here with back knee under the back hip, until the knees close up on ball release in tent peg 3

You're looking to take advantage of your shoulder-hip separation, by creating a stretch reflex where your arm is out behind you, meaning your hips and shoulders are apart from each other. If it is correct it will be automatically snapped forwards as your hips and shoulders snap back into alignment.

People often describe this as a 'slingshot' effect but that's confusing because it makes it sound like you are a "slinger" and implies that only the likes of Malinga or Shoaib Akhtar achieve speed in this way. In fact, every fast bowler uses this stretch reflex to a certain extent.

Who does the drop step?

Every fast bowler should do it, but doesn't. However, look in particular at Shoaib Akhtar, Mitchell Johnson and Brett Lee. Akthar at times got his trailing knee very low. Lee had his about 6 inches from the turf. Lee's 'drop-step front-foot block' is porbably the best I have seen. But all use the technique of hip-shoulder separation to power their action, with Akhtar's being especially good and partly explaining why he could bowl and maintain such high speeds.

Shoaib Akhtar, for example, did not always have a fully straight front leg when he bowled but his use of the hip-shoulder separation and the resulting stretch reflex is about the best there is: he gets his bowling arm right behind his head and as his front foot lands, his body and his bowling arm are driven forwards with great power.

What to do

Land softly with your back foot - not hard as most coaches tell you: you don't want to stop dead and lose the momentum of your run-up. You are then looking to drag your back foot through the crease for as long as you can through your action. Keep your front leg straight, so that it hits the ground quite hard. Just before it does, bend your back knee. As your back leg comes through, with your back foot dragging along the ground, your knees will come level with each other and your hips will shoot forward.

Walking it through

You can walk this though now, at home. With your standing back leg (foot pointing forward) step with your front foot (straight leg) and start to bend your back knee. As your front foot hits the floor, drag your back foot on your toes and eventually your knees will be level with each other: your bent back leg is pulled through, as your bowling arm comes over. Your knees will be level as your arm comes over, meaning your hips are now facing forwards. Instead of thinking of an (unrealistically) 'high' action, you are creating extra power from this consciously lower position as you bend forward at the hips.

In Practice

Javelin throwers throw with their legs. And a big part of my coaching is to encourage bowlers to do the same when they bowl because that is where the power will come from. Javelin throwing is all about maximising power through technique. The last thing a javelin thrower does is throw the javelin and the last thing a fast bowler does is bowl the ball: everything else has to be in place first.

The vast majority of fast bowlers who come to me, especially young fast bowlers, have concentrated on their upper-body and on getting speed from their shoulders and arms. This means they are missing out on all the extra power that can be achieved by making sure feet, knees and hips are providing the right base for the action.

The principles for the drop-step front-foot block are the same as in javelin: the only difference is that a javelin thrower is looking to launch it over 80-90m into the air whereas a cricketer has to land the ball within 20m. And, after working on the drop step, you may find yourself bowling a very full length with your extra power at first. Those who try to get extra pace *purely* **from their arm** often end up bowling too short.

It is highly desirable to collapse your back leg after impact so you can drive all your energy into your block. If you land hard on back foot impact you will lose much of your ground speed and begin to 'push' your top half forward too soon to actually bowl. So you want to have a very soft step or 'drop step' where all your weight transfers efficiently into your block.

The secret is to keep your back knee immediately below your back hip through your action and this is done by having a feeling of stepping down. If you get the drop step correct, you will discover that your knee is only just above your ankle (in an 'L' shape) as your bowling arm comes over to bowl. You will find that it is easiest to do this when you keep your back foot fully on the floor (dragging) right up until release of the ball.

Again, it is important that you keep your knee low (drop step) and back foot dragging to ensure your hips are level into the bowling action and provide a stable base. The foot dragging helps keep the hip flexors engaged into the block and stops you bowling of one leg like you are doing the highland fling. The only bowlers who lift their back foot before releasing the ball should be spinners.

Watch a javelin thrower, baseball pitcher, boxer throw a punch, or other power generation sports and you will see the back foot is in contact right up to release of that power. You wouldn't throw a ball off one leg, play a cover drive off one leg or punch off one leg. Don't bowl off one leg either. Learn how to keep your hip flexor engaged by dragging the foot and driving the hips hard to target. It feels like taking a penalty kick in rugby or free kick in football, but not lifting the kicking foot.

FRONT FOOT BLOCK

The bottom line is if you bend your front leg when you bowl, you will lose the ability to transfer all your base energy into your top half. The idea is you want to decelerate your bottom half to accelerate your top half.

The front leg will be locked out so the hip on your bowling side can rotate against the front hip. Your front leg and hip thus act somewhat like the hinges on a door – creating a solid position for the bowling side to drive hard against. And you want this straight leg to be angled back against your hips. You don't want to be standing up tall. In fact I want you to think the opposite. Your leg will be angle back against your legs so that when you bowl with your chest driven forward, there is a 90 degree bend at the waist. This is known as the power blast.

Imagine being in a car without seatbelts travelling at speed. If you hit a wall, the car stops but you keep going. You want to hit the brakes hard with your front foot block to achieve this. Come to a sudden stop with the front leg angled back so your hips can be driven hard against it.

The tendency for many people is to roll forward before the hips have rotated and to finish with their weight on your front foot. This sliding forward of the hips robs you of power. The hips don't rotate the way they should to free up your bowling arm. They can't as they're too busy sliding forward and then get stuck supporting all of your weight on top of your front leg – it's really hard for your hips to rotate if that's going on.

Against a blocked, straight front leg, you can rotate your hips and drive your knee so that on release of the ball, your knees will close. The back foot remains in contact until you let the ball go

In a similar way, the potential energy you have generated, plus the ground speed of your run up into your front foot block, adds to the rotational force of your hips driving and front arm pulling against the locked front leg. You can begin to see where the ball speed is now coming from. And all of this is happening ahead of the last thing you do when you bowl – actually let the ball go.

You are looking to create angles so you transfer the power up the body – from the ground, into your legs, through your hips, into your chest, then shoulders, into your bowling arm and finally into the ball.

It works like a 5 stage rocket. A rocket moves in stages with each stage accelerating the next one and so on until maximum speed is achieved. You will use all the forces in your body to 'ripple' the power by the muscle sequencing, so the ball can be delivered at full pace.

STRETCH REFLEX

It is at this point I want to mention the stretch reflex (arm pull) of the bowling arm.

By delaying the arm pull or at least having a feeling of a 'slingshot' you create maximum range of motion. Think about something for a moment. When you bowl a cricket ball you move your arm from behind you to in front of you, through a range of less than two metres. Yet in that range, you accelerate a ball up to 70, 80 or even 90 mph. It happens in fractions of seconds. There is no car on the planet can do that or move that fast. And all the time you are holding onto the ball it is accelerating. Because the instant you let it go, it is slowing down. Gravity and wind resistance slow the ball as it leaves your hand. It makes sense then to hang onto the ball as long as possible. Or in other words, increase your range of motion. The shorter your arm pull, the smaller the range of motion.

This is the start of the Stretch Reflex and drop step. By taking the arm fully backwards as the body moves forwards, a hip/shoulder separation is caused that accelerates the bowling arm in a 'reflex' of the muscles rapidly contracting when the front foot blocks. The hips lead the shoulders through as the top stays 'neutral'

The other thing that happens when you 'delay' the bowling arm slightly is you create hip drive through something called shoulder hip separation (Pic page 39). This is where the hips lead the upswing of the arm and you get a catapult effect. Hips create the extra 'oomph' you seek. This is done in conjunction with the front arm pull.

The big muscles, your hips and the core of your torso do all the work here. The arm is just along for the ride, for the most part. After a fast bowling session, if you end up with sore muscles, you are likely to be sore in your hips and obliques (outside stomach muscles). If you are experiencing soreness in your shoulder and triceps, you are most likely not using enough big muscles or you are trying too hard with your arm. It doesn't help. Good strong, fast arm movement is a key portion of the technique, so it's not totally without effort, it is just that tons of effort should not be placed there – too much arm is a problem.

You will understand now that your hips are the most important part of your body when generating speed. There is something in the human body called the hidden force multiplier. Simply put it shows that by increasing hip rotation speed, you can increase your arm speed up to ten times. That means, 1 mph on the hips can equal up to 10 mph on the arm speed. In the same way you make a toy propeller fly by turning the shaft and not the blade, you can accelerate your bowling arm speed by increasing the movement, range and speed of your hips.

This is done by rotating the hips so that when the ball is released from your hand, you are facing totally front on. You will have discovered in *The Fast Bowler's Bible* that every bowler is front on when they release a cricket ball. It means that if you land sideways in tent peg 1 then your bowling hip will rotate 90 degrees (range of motion), compared to a midway bowler (45 degrees) or a front on bowler (already hips facing forward).

This goes some way to explaining why a side on version of a bowler, compared to a front on version of a bowler, will be faster. This is assuming everything else worked correctly in sequence. And we know from the hidden force multiplier that having highly active hips that move through a large range of motion at great speed, will generate a huge amount of pace.

TENT PEG THREE

I personally feel this is the most important position in the bowling action and one that is vital to maintaining maximum speed from the body. Tent Peg 3 happens on the instant of release of the cricket ball from a bowler's hand. This is also where we use the front foot plant mentioned in tent peg 2 to it's fullest.
How you let the cricket ball go affects how the ball behaves. Whether it is wrist postion, arm height or speed, the position at release of the ball is key.

Tent Peg Three

You will see from the images above how the perfect tent peg 3 position should look. And there are various factors at play to achieve it.

Against a braced front leg you will find that the top half of the body flexes forward and the bowling hand delivers the ball from above the bowling shoulder and bowling hip. Your chest is facing the batsman, your hips are too. From the stretch reflex position, the shoulder catches the hips up to make an accelerated release of the ball like a catapult. You will see that even though this is a power blast position, the body is very balanced.

The release of the ball itself happens above or *ahead of* the front foot. This is highly desirable. That's because the longer you hold on to the cricket ball, the more it is accelerating. For every split second you are powering the ball forwards, it is accelerating. This is why it makes sense to hang on to the cricket ball for as long as possible. The moment you release the ball, it starts to slow down.

To get this you will need to be in an advanced shoulder position, fully extended, and driven towards your target. Don't let the ball go until you have maximised your power arm stretch reflex.

Your shoulders (and left and right hand sides) will be fully synchronised by utilising the front arm pull correctly, which I will outline in more detail in a moment.

MYTH BUSTER – "STAND UP AND GET MORE BOUNCE"

This is still very popular with coaches I am sad to say. Getting a few centimetres 'taller' in the action does not make the difference to the bounce of a cricket ball.

If you imagine the angle of trajectory and pitching of a cricket ball, then you will know that what makes a ball bounce higher is the SPEED at which it hits the turf. A ball fired in from a bowling machine or fast bowler at 95 mph will bounce significantly more compared to a ball bowled at 60 mph - a ball bowled from either 1.88m compared to 1.92m, really will not. However, if it was bowled from 2.92m I would agree, but we are not talking about an extra metre here. A tall bowler can get more bounce than a short bowler, but *standing* taller does not make a significant difference.

The second thing that is wrong about 'standing tall' when you bowl is you lose the power positions described here in tent peg 3, which are the keys to bowling faster and straighter.

So not only is it completely the wrong advice to get a bowler to stand up to get more bounce, it actually makes them slower, which of course gives them less bounce. Lack of speed (not bowler height) is why a spinner's short delivery is not a bouncer.

FRONT ARM PULL

The front arm here is also important. That's because the front arm and the bowling arm are connected through the shoulders and by rotating the shoulders fully at the right time, we can add some MPH to the ball.

Grab the batsman's collar and pull it towards you, so your elbow drives hard behind you. This move accelerates your bowling shoulder and also helps you to line your shoulders correctly for the release of the ball

MYTH BUSTER – "PULL YOUR FRONT ARM DOWN LIKE A TOILET CHAIN"

I want to address something about the front arm that I hear perpetuated by some coaches. And that is "pull your front arm down like a toilet chain". There are many issues with this move:

1. Your shorten your arm too early
2. You drive downwards with your non-bowling shoulder
3. You put a great deal of 'crunching' down into your intercostals
4. Your bowling shoulder doesn't move forwards

Sit there for a moment as you read this and lift your non bowling arm high and then drive your elbow down like you are pulling a toilet chain from above your head. Now see if your other shoulder moves at all. Nothing, nada, zilch.

Now reach your non bowling arm out straight (like you are patting someone on the head) and pull your elbow back behind you (as if you are elbowing someone). Now see if your other shoulder moves at all. Yep, you cannot HELP but have some forward rotation of the bowling shoulder.

So we can easily show that the CORRECT movement for **R**ange of motion, **S**eparation, **S**peed, **S**equencing and **A**lignment (**RSSSA**), is to 'throw' the non bowling hand at the batsman then pull it hard from in front of you, by then elbowing behind you - and NOT up to down, as with a toilet chain.

You will recall in tent peg 2 that your front arm was s-t-r-e-t-c-h-e-d out to grab the batsman's collar. As soon as you feel the front foot plant, this is your cue to pull hard against your braced front leg. You should not be pulling your front arm too early (without front foot impacted) because you need the ground to pull against. The front leg braced provides this. You can spot an inefficient front arm position by looking at a sideways image of front foot impact on a fast bowler and seeing if the bowling arm is still above the waist or not. Above the waist or close to it and the pull is happening at the correct time – below the waist or straight down and the arm has been pulled against fresh air (no base). This is known as 'losing the front arm' and the vast majority of bowlers do it.

MYTH BUSTER – "BRUSH YOUR EAR"

When it comes to the height of the bowling arm, as I said in The Fast Bowler's Bible, "you can bowl any hour before 12, but not a minute past". If you put your bowling arm up above you so it is comfortable, you will find that far from 'brushing your ear' it is likely to be above the end of your shoulder. This gives you a between 11 and 12 o'clock release position and that is perfectly natural.

Two reasons why brushing your ear is just really appalling advice to any fast bowler.

Firstly, it easily tips you past the wrong side of your body and you can start your upswing of your bowling arm outside your body width. This is bowling 'in to out' and if you track the ball in your hand it 'loops'. Secondly, your wrist position is likely to be completely wrong because you will feel as if you are pushing the ball at the batsman, rather than pulling it.

If you recall that all fast bowlers are front on when they bowl, just have a think as you sit there, which side of your body your bowling hand is? That's the side you should bowl from. Keep it natural, normal, and simple

It doesn't make you a poor bowler if you do this. It simply means you haven't used the full rotational power pull in your front arm at the right time.

So we can see the timing of this is important. What is also important is how you pull it. It is important to bear in mind that things happen in fractions of seconds and getting a feel for them is extremely difficult. But understanding what is working and when can give you a huge advantage when it comes to training and practice. As you pull your elbow back against a braced front leg, you will also drive your chest towards the batsman. This 'chest drive' almost comes naturally because when you plant your front foot into the ground you are rapidly decelerating your bottom half, and that energy has to go somewhere. You want it to be transferred into your top half. The sensation is as if someone has literally shoved you in the back. And there would be good reason for that.

It is a series of movements, highly efficient and complex, that multiply your speed sequentially, to create maximum arm speed so you can bowl the ball quickly.

MOST COMMON MISTAKES

Bending the front leg

The front leg 'ram rod' is the principle of taking ground speed and transferring it into the top half of the action so the ball can be delivered quickly. Should a bowler's front leg buckle then the energy will stop at the knee and travel no further. We wish to create a straight leg so energy can ripple like a domino effect through the hips and into the ball.

Not closing up the knees

One of the most important things in creating pace is hip drive and rotation. If the knees are left open like this they still have some way to drive before the ball is bowled. The knees should pass each other at the exact point of release showing the top and bottom half of the action is totally synchronized. A bowler who doesn't use their legs correctly is relying on the top half to bowl – thus missing a large part of what creates speed.

Releasing the ball over wrong hip or 'past midnight'

The golden rule is "any hour before midnight but not a minute past" when it comes to releasing the ball relative to the perpendicular. The resultant lean creates a difficult wrist position and a feel of pushing the cricket ball. Many bowlers who are called for throwing all seem to get into this position.

Apart from creating a lateral flexion that can have injury issues in the back or side, a bowler can have real difficulties swinging the ball away. A severe lateral flexion is one of the problems associated with stress fractures of the spine and ideally should be corrected as a soon as possible.

Splayed front foot

Apart from being somewhat uncomfortable, this position can create injuries in the knee and ligaments. Some of the typical problems can also occur around the ankle area and achilles, too. The misalignment of the foot means that the angle of the base of the action is compromised. A bowler can often follow the foot angle on their follow through and finish with a shoulder rotation towards second slip. If you remember your feet are your 'tyres' then you would ideally want those to be travelling towards the target and not away from it.

Having bowling hip higher than non bowling hip

The idea is to have a stable hip position on release of the ball and this means trying to maintain a level line between the bowling hip and the non-bowling hip. If a bowler has a good drop step like Brett Lee for example, they will have stable hips and be able to use the hip drive correctly into the front foot block. As with lateral flexion (lean away) this position tilts the body offline. It's a sign of little or no drop step in the action.

Lifting the back foot off the ground

Great for spinners, rubbish for fast bowlers. If you want to feel what it's like to lose power, stand in front of a wall with your legs split and push against it then lift your back foot off the ground. Fast bowlers want to keep their back foot in contact into the release of the ball (by dragging) and maintaining a hip flexor drive of the hip. The foot remains engaged and only lifts into tent peg four after you have let go of the ball. To use the front foot block, get low into it and bowl against the front leg, not over it. The top half of the body makes a 90 degree angle against the locked out front leg. To "stand up and bowl tall" loses all that transferred energy. 'Hit' the block hard and drive the hips like a door shutting fast against a door hinge.

TENT PEG FOUR

Tent Peg Four

If you have ensured the previous tent pegs are all in place, it is almost inevitable that tent peg four will be correct. That's because the finishing position of the bowling action is a consequence of what has gone before. The follow through is a reaction to what has preceded it. And you can learn a great deal from a follow through.

As you go through into tent peg four, your exit stride from the crease, you are attempting to maintain all of your forward momentum towards the target. This is where your shoulders have fully rotated, your arms have pulled through hard and your back leg drives upwards at the knee to keep your base moving in a straight line. The issue for many bowlers' transition from tent peg three at release of the ball, is they feel their job is done. However, it is by developing a DEEP chest drive, where the back levels out like a surf board, and a strong knee drive, that we ensure the top and bottom half of the body COMPLETES the action, or 'finishes off'.

Starting with the bowling hand first to give you an idea, it is best to try to have this hand go past the top of your front leg sock. When you are in that sort of extension through the action you will find your back will be close to parallel to the floor. This hand then finishes up under your non-bowling armpit, which also guarantees you have a full bowling shoulder rotation.

What will assist you in this finish is the non-bowling arm being released from tent peg three (pulled in to your side), being released upwards so the finger tips of that hand 'touch the sky' up behind you. The two hands effectively then both finish pointing or at least driving, upwards towards the sky from a level back.

Your head will follow the ball down and so therefore take your bodyweight directly towards off stump. If you feel you are grabbing onto the side netting in a practice session, or running towards cover point on your follow through, the chances are your head is going that way as you come out of the crease.

MOST COMMON MISTAKES

Pivoting on the front foot like a spinner

The problem here is evident as the feet are effectively the tyres of the body and show exactly where the energy is going. It is more than likely created by a bowler who 'crosses' their feet over (front foot across the body compared to back foot) and could lead to a loss of pace as well as additional stress. This looks more like a spinner bowling than a pace bowler.

Not driving top half through straight

This is a clear sign that a bowler's energy is not going towards the target.

The top half of the action dictates where the ball is trying to go so any movement not directly at the top of off stump from the base can affect the accuracy of the ball release. Often a player will 'twist' the top half as they bowl around their body and this can misalign the release meaning that a bowler will have to compensate somewhere else in the action.

Not completing shoulder rotation

Both hands should finish high and pointing upwards. To achieve this a bowler will have a full shoulder rotation with the bowling shoulder driving down into the floor in front of the bowler. The image is a sign that the bowler hasn't 'completed' the bowling action with a strong chest drive. The top half of the body would be parallel to the ground like a surf board and the head would be at hip level.

Not holding a strong finish (swimming)

When your non-bowling arm completes, it shouldn't come forward again as if you are swimming. This is because you want to fully 'finish' the shoulders off and the act of 'swimming' means you have not completed correctly. Your bowling shoulder should be driving down into the ground and turned towards the batter - not upright and coming out of your action.

Bowling knee not driving out straight

This is a sign that either the knee has over rotated or the back foot is coming around the front leg. It can affect the power out of the action and also create issues in a bowler's knee if the twisting occurs at that part. The top half has to work very hard to keep the action aligned.

8

Not So Simple Forces At Play, Made Easy

I want to get **way** less technical than I should. That's because when you bowl there are things like inertia, force, mass, acceleration, equal reactive forces, potential and kinetic energy plus a whole bunch of overly technical phraseology that very few of us need to understand. And whilst it gets the boffins excited, it doesn't help us as bowlers or coaches to know this stuff, trust me.

We don't need to get into applied biomechanics too deeply to explain it.

But it's also why, when anyone asks "why do some people bowl fast and others don't?" it cannot be answered by the ridiculous statement 'fast bowlers are born". Or suggesting it is all about diet, pitch conditions, genetics or other factors that are socio-economical.

All you need to understand is why things work and what you can do about making them better. When you appreciate there is a process to fast bowling and we can learn it, then you will start to understand that those who claim they can coach fast bowling because they used to play at such and such a level, are misguided. Genuine face palm moments.

So when it comes to how the body generates speed, we need to take a simplistic look at the forces at play so you can get an understanding of how to and why you bowl the speed you do. This will have the experts crying into their legumes.

To keep it very simple, and use my own terminology there are three main forces: rotational, linear and reactive. You use all three to bowl with.

ROTATIONAL

Rotational force is the force created by joints rotating and moving so that energy can be transferred. If you swing your arm around for example, you will appreciate you can bowl a ball by simply sitting down. Ankles, knees, hips, shoulders and a whole host of other body parts, move in synchronization to generate force.

LINEAR

This is force created by movement along a linear path such as run up, arm pull, chest drive and knee drive for example. Moving along the line (or against it to create a stretch) uses your energy and creates a force, through a range of motion.

REACTIVE

This force is created by moving against the ground or your own body to generate a force to propel the cricket ball. As an example, the front foot block makes the most of this in particular and the resultant feeling is a 'jolt' through the top half.

If we take you all the way back to RSSSA at the beginning you will start to appreciate what body parts are moving to apply the forces to the best effect.

It is from this knowledge base that the book was written. That's why the successful transformation from the skill drills, go with making the speed and accuracy of the bowlers as efficient as possible.

So how exactly should you do the skill drills?

9

Fast or Slow?

There is a fundamental rule of fast bowling coaching. You do not have a snowball in the desert's chance of making changes to your action when bowling to batsmen in nets, or from a full run up with a ball in your hand.

I have seen countless coaches attempt to offer advice to fast bowlers when they are 'under pressure' in nets or when thinking about where the ball goes (outcomes). You cannot begin to change a small part of your bowling action (alignment and sequencing) if you are worried where the ball is going. It's simple common sense.

The ONLY way you can work through your action is to do isolation drills and break apart the movements to look at them.

But more than this for accelerated learning, you will understand the movements if you do them in SUPER slow motion. When you go through the movements as slowly as you can you begin to feel what muscles are working and when. I can only recommend that you move through the positions you wish to get into, without a ball in your hand and also by looking in a mirror when you do them. You will start to see and feel the changes you want to make by literally feeling the motions you are making.

What you then do is build those movements up so they happen slightly faster. Over time, you then increase those speeds to get closer to a bowling speed.

Later on in this book, we will explain exactly how that is done and what you need to think about when drilling. Because ultimately, it will be both the quality of your drills plus how you understand what you are doing, that will lead to solid changes and improvements in your skill levels.

Get rid of the ball from your hand before you attempt to overwrite your muscle memory. Your brain will try to resist by implementing what it knows to be natural. You need to be able to overlay new information in a precise way and doing it slowly, without the hinderence of cricket, is the starting point for change.

10

Statics, Walk-Throughs, Jog-Throughs, Run-Throughs

Change takes time.

Like expecting a plant to grow, you wouldn't constantly be looking to see if there is any difference after just a short while. Your action is like that plant. It takes many 'waterings' and little change before you begin to even notice something is happening. And the change might be extremely small. So you need to show some tremendous patience. But the good news is you can do correction drills and tweaks to your action at any time of the year. You don't have to wait for the season to end, or to be injured, or wait for the 'right time'. Your optimum time for making improvements is NOW.

The mistake coaches often make is to say that a bowler shouldn't be 'messing around' with their bowling action during the season.

This is wrong on two levels. Firstly, making positive tweaks and corrections, isn't 'messing around'. Batsmen constantly review their batting and if any technical changes need to be worked on, a coach will often do that. Secondly, if you were on the wrong road driving, you wouldn't just carry on - you would make adjustments to reach your destination. So simply leaving something alone to reinforce mistakes that go unchecked is clearly madness.

Your practices and down time from matches are the times to work on any technical changes. Once the matches resume, **you just carry on bowling as normal**. This is the trick. You simply cannot be thinking technically when you are playing cricket, because matches are ONLY about outcomes. The scorebook shows runs, maidens, overs and wickets - there is no column that says 'how good is my action'. That's why we work technically hard AWAY from matches, not IN them. And for good reason, too. Your technique is your servant and when you cross the white line to play your match, you want your servant to be with you, looking after you, helping you to be fast and accurate under pressure. You don't want to feel all alone, with little or no idea what you are doing.

Great technique gives you supreme confidence. The one thing most players report after working on their action is they feel so much more confident in what they are doing when it counts. Results improve. Stats get better. People start to notice things about you. And this is a huge win-win because you start then to up-skill yourself as a bowler and become far more consistent.

If you plan to change *anything*, take it in bite-sized pieces. As we found in the "chunking" part of the technical aspects of coaching, it is only by experiencing changes in small movements through isolating them, that we will be able to get a feel for what is actually going on. You cannot feel anything at high speed because the movements are way too fast and complex to truly appreciate what is going on, and possibly going wrong.

To start off, place yourself into the correct positions you want to achieve and simply get a feel for those positions. You are trying to fast track those positions into your brain and you have to focus on understanding what the kinesthetics of each movement you make, is like.

It would make sense if you have access to a video camera at this point to keep a record of what you are doing and to see yourself in review. If you want to start off by filming your existing bowling action and then possibly going through it in slow motion. You will see very many things lost when you view it at normal speed. You can then at a later date, compare and contrast your 'new' action and changes you are practicing.

You need to get extremely fussy with those positions, too. Because the truth is if you cannot get into the right action when you are static, you have little chance at full speed, off your full run, with a ball in your hand and a batter waiting. So take your time. Be precise.

Don't accept less than 100%

And do not do any of the drills at this stage with a cricket ball. You don't need a cricket ball. You are merely grooving your muscle memory to ultimately 'recall' the positions without you having to consciously think about them.

I suggest you try to further detach yourself from the memory of bowling by doing the initial drills 'out of context'. This means not using a crease, lines, stumps or anything else that can hijack your system into thinking you are bowling.

Instead, we wish to create an environment that your mind cannot object to and this can be done by working in any area other than a crease. To simulate a bowling action so we can CHANGE it, we seek to fool the mind into accepting the new movements as non-threatening to your existing action. So as you do your static drills, ensure you are feeling like it's a new sport you are learning. This will help.

Just HOLDING the key positions will help you balance correctly and maintain an even position. When it comes to simulating the 4 tent pegs for instance, this is exactly the way to start off.

Once you master each position you then move on to joining movements together

How you join those movements is your *style* or your own way of doing it. Everyone will have a different way. How you move through each phase of your action is the *style* - and the content of the technique is the *substance*. There is always a trade-off between style and substance. A bowler's action can often 'look nice' because it is flowing yet is riddled with technical flaws that stop that bowler from becoming a top class cricketer. Another bowler might have a 'jerky' or 'awkward' looking action yet that masks some tremendous biomechanics that create express pace, power and control.

The truth is everyone has their own way of bowling dependent upon back foot position right through to the finish of the action. The idea is to identify clearly what aspects you wish to alter and then build those in - very slowly.

As you get more confident and comfortable with what you are doing you move into a walk-through drill. This is as it sounds, a drill where you walk up into the action and then put all your positions together into one, flowing movement. But here's the problem:

1. When you walk-through it feels weird
2. You cannot focus on all the positions simultaneously
3. You can be off balance
4. Your back foot often lands in the wrong position

Don't worry about any of this. The entire point of you building any drill up is to start making changes and **changes begin the moment you think about them**. The secret is to start *feeling* what's right and wrong. You are about to become your own coach and as well as be the eyes & ears of what you are doing, you also need to instantly feedback to yourself so you can continually adjust.

The golden rule is, if the action starts to break down or fall apart, or you start to lose the key positions, then **GO BACK TO THE POINT WHERE IT WAS PERFECT** and start again from there.

This is true for any level of drill you do, and for all disciplines.

The walk through gives you a fraction more ground speed, which will enable your bottom half to drive a bit faster. This engages the hips and legs better, plus synchronises the overall movement. The faster you move in your approach, the more ground speed you have to transfer into the speed of the ball.

Now when you move on to a jog-through where you take a very light jog, you will start to jump at the crease a small amount and your foot patterning will change. That's because your feet move quicker and with a small jump, you start to initiate hang time. This will give a slight delay as you would get when you bowl. Bear this in mind.

A run through drill will be the closest drill you have to bowling but not actually doing so. You can and should still try to be aware of the technical parts in a way that you cannot when you are bowling for real. It does feel mighty odd to bowl without a ball from virtually a full run up. That's because you are probably thinking about the tent pegs yet have other issues like take-off, hang time and run-up to contend with.

Don't worry about those at this stage. The only purpose of run through drills is to create additional ground speed to synchronise the top and bottom half of your bowling action. As we discovered earlier, if you tend to bowl short in a match it usually means your top half is too active and if you bowl too full, your legs are moving too fast for your top half. So bowling without a ball allows you the latitude to play around with the timings so that you feel a co-ordinated release.

11

Isolation & Stripped-Out Drills

The great thing about doing isolation drills is you can do them for any and all parts of your bowling. You can make up your own effectively. That's because you are trying to replicate what you want to do, in an isolated way.

For example, if you wish to practice your take off from your run up into your action, then just run and drill that particular part until it is exactly what you want. You would run, jump and then just 'bail out' of your action. What I mean by that is you don't bother actually bowling because you are simply working the jumping part of your bowling.

The same goes for run-up, load-up, hand positions, foot positions - in fact all parts of your cricket can be isolated, stripped out and then worked on. That is the beauty of doing this type of drill.

You have to remember though that it does feel very different when you complete movements at slower speeds and it will make you extremely aware of those movements, too.

When you are working on your tent peg positions, you should get comfortable with each of them in turn before attempting to link them together. If you want to know if you have that linking correct, attempt them in a *reverse* order. Should you be able to go backwards and forwards in your action and STILL understand what you are doing then you will have truly worked out the mechanics of your movements in the crease.

Often the changes are so small as to almost be unnoticable. But they sometimes feel very big. Whenever you make a change, because that change may be completely different to the way you have done it before, it feels different. Others might look at it and think it looks exactly the same. So there is a trade-off between what it feels like and what it looks like. The bigger the changes, clearly the bigger the visual differences you will see. This is why you should recall that small keys open big locks.

The other thing about stripped out drills is by isolating the upper body and the lower body in your foundational power bowling drills, you can really develop the performance of these parts of your body.

The near impossible challenge you face when trying to assemble all of the pieces at once becomes much easier when you reduce the criteria and focus on one thing at a time. The whole body is moving: hands, arms, feet, legs, hips, torso, shoulders, and everything in between. These pieces of your body work in concert, and in order to work in concert, they must also function solo.

That is the key to making any drills you do, work.

It is important to note that bowling fast is not a single day lesson. It takes several sessions to learn the techniques and several to start applying them. You have to choose your battles while learning and teaching it. Go for simple wins first, the things you find easiest to master.

12
Cross Over Sessions

After doing a huge amount of drills, changes, tweaks and other things to change your muscle memory, there comes a time when you have to put it all together, with a ball in your hand, and then deliver it. Up until now though, you have learned not to worry about anything except your body positions.

This is exactly correct. But you are about to enter a world of confusion and dreadful outcomes as you start to 'bowl' again whilst being conscious of what you are doing. This is known as a 'cross over' session, where you cross over from technical (action) to tactical (outcomes) but still think about the technical.

Now I can assure you this is a truly horrible session. You will feel everything that is happening and you will feel it is wrong most likely. That's because you are engaging BOTH the conscious and sub-conscious parts of your brain when you only do the conscious in drills and subconscious in matches/outcomes.

By waking *both* parts of the brain, you are now going to bash them into one another with the resultant experience being one of confusion and downright weirdness. **This is a necessary step**.

You want to adjust to crossing over so your subconscious takes charge of your action, as it does in a match. Before it can take charge, you have to hold its hand by telling it what you want to happen and you do this by still thinking about your technique.

The best way to run a session like this is to have a target set up, preferably on the top of off stump, and look at that with the aim of hitting it, whilst being extremely aware of the action. You now have to balance whether it is more important to be able to hit the target or more important to have your technical aspect hold up. Before you hand the baton over to your subconscious and just let it take over, you must try to keep the integrity of the action as a priority.

You should film this session and then review the footage.

The first cross over session is the worst. The next time you revisit it you will find it is somewhat easier. And the more you are able to put this type of session together, the better your action will 'feel'. Once you have experienced it you will know exactly what I am talking about.

When you get to the point you can pretty much maintain the correct positions and still hit the areas you want, it is time to pass the whole thing across to outcomes and simply bowl. This is the moment your action will have changed.

Please understand that anything can be changed at any time. It is only by serious repetitions that we alter those things that feel natural to us.

If you feel parts of your bowling need work you can go back to tent pegs or other isolation and stripped out drills any time you wish to tidy them up.

13
General Training For Optimal Results
8 Principles You Need To Know

This section is for those of you with a more than keen interest in overall fitness training and how to make the very best of your physical attributes. Only read this if you wish to understand the PRINCIPLES behind the training as it doesn't include the *actual* training exercises itself for very good reasons; everyone is different, I don't know how old you are and I don't know what fitness level you are already at.

That's why I don't wish to get massively technical here. But I do want to get you thinking about what you can do to help yourself (or those you coach) to become a far better fast bowler. Because the truth is, unless you are part of a world-class training programme, the chances are you will have to do much of the work yourself to support your own physical development.

Also a list of 'ideal, simple exercises' was covered somewhat in *The Fast Bowler's Bible*. Instead, I am going to get you to think and consider "how can I help myself?" and "what should I be looking at?" when it comes to making yourself as ready as possible. I urge you to research and discover for yourself what's out there.

So here I am going to talk about 8 principles, either for you or the players you work with:

The Overload Principle

The Balance Principle

The Individualisation Principle

The Transfer Principle

The Specifics Principle

The Recovery Principle

The Reversibility Principle

The Variation Principle

These are principles that will help you to understand training, and the importance strength & conditioning plays in making you a better cricketer. Read this if you wish to get a deeper knowledge in this area, but use it purely as a *guide* and not a definitive answer.

THE OVERLOAD PRINCIPLE

The Overload Principle is a basic sports fitness training concept. It means that in order to improve, fast bowlers must continually work harder as their bodies adjust to existing workouts. Overloading also plays a role in skill learning.

Improving cardiovascular fitness involves keeping moderate activities for extended periods of time. Increasing strength requires lifing increasingly heavier weight loads. The principle applies to length and amount of training, as well.

For example, if your goal is to improve upper body strength, you would continue to increase training weight loads until your goal was achieved.

If the training load was not increased to push you to higher levels of strength, you would show little improvement. To improve your cricket by increased upper body strength for example, must be merged into whole body execution of game skills.

Overload and Cricket Skill Learning

Cricket skills are learned through a variety of techniques and concepts. It is the **quality of practice** that counts, rather than quantity and intensity.

Learning movements correctly the first time is ideal. But when learned skills require substantial corrections, overlearning helps.

Overlearning means repeatedly practicing a skill beyond what is required to perform it. Simply, it is a method where quality and quantity are used to overcome errors. Normally, skills are best learned when fatigue does not affect the cricketer's ability to correctly pattern movements.

Tips on Applying the Overload Principle

The following advice is commonly accepted and practiced. Think about your own training and what you wish to achieve:

1. Increase loads gradually and progressively. Training loads should become more intense over a period of time, not increased too abruptly or with too much intensity.

2. Test maximums. Through testing, even if the test comes in the form of competition, training loads usually vary between 60-85% of maximum efforts.

3. Avoid muscular failure. It is not necessary to train until muscles fail or the player collapses.

4. Allow ample recovery time. Too little recovery over time can cause an overtraining effect. Too much recovery time can cause a detraining effect.

5. Plan and monitor training loads. Design long-range, periodised training programmes, test players, and evaluate their progress to guide training decisions about overload.

6. Monitor team and individual progress. Identify general areas where there are common deficits compared to other fitness components and skill qualities. If players "run out of gas", for example, training can be overloaded to improve skilled performances when fatigued.

7. Alternate activities. Organise workouts to allow recovery on some aspects of training while increasing intensity on others. Use periodised planning to link into weekly and daily activities.

8. Coordinate all training activities and schedules. Fitness training loads should be adjusted for technical and tactical activities, travel, competitions, and other factors that could influence how overloading should occur. This would include 'tapering' that refers to the practice of reducing exercise in the days just before an important competition.

9. Focus on skill work first. Practice skills that require greater coordination prior to intense fitness training if both are performed in the same workout session. For example, complete Olympic lifting before weight training activities of lesser complexity.

The Overload Principle must work in concert with other Sports Training Principles. None of these principles work in isolation fully unless they blend with:

THE BALANCE PRINCIPLE

The Balance Principle dictates that all training must be properly proportioned in order to achieve best results. This broad principle operates at many levels of human performance. **All things in moderation** applies to sports training as well as life, in general.

This principle suggests the right mix of training activities, diet, and healthy lifestyle habits. Going to extremes can result in poor performance, illness, and injury.

Coaching Tips to Promote an Optimal Training Balance

1. Training Activities. Design your total training programme to include the proper proportions of activities and time allocated to develop them. This is a basic goal of the annual programme plan.

2. Training Intensity. "More is better" style of thinking may not produce the best results. Then again, undertraining will not promote adequate progress. Find the best balance of intensity and recovery. Be sensitive to signs of overtraining in your players.

3. Muscle Balancing. Opposing muscle strength should fall within certain ranges. Not all muscles should be worked the same. For example, hamstrings should be 60-75% of the strength of the quadriceps. The very nature of sport movements can promote imbalances. Training should include flexibility, muscle testing, and balancing to prevent injuries.

4. Body Composition. Achieving the best balance of body fat vs. lean body mass is important. Monitoring body mass index can help guide dietary and training decisions.

5. Nutrition. Players' diets must include essential nutrients in proper proportions that may shift depending upon physical demands. Lack of proper nutrients (e.g., iron, protein) can slow progress. Monitoring food intake and supplements can help players achieve best results.

6. Evaluation. Evaluating various aspects of players' health and performance can assist in identifying areas where imbalances may occur and what is needed to correct them.

THE INDIVIDUALISATION PRINCIPLE

The Individualisation Principle dictates that training should be adjusted according to each cricketer's needs, such as age, gender, rate of progress, and previous experience. The goal of individualisation is to capitalise on each cricketer's strengths and minimise the effects of their shortcomings.

Training programme revisions for individual players can come in many forms. Adjustments can be made for skill level, size, medical conditions, injuries, motivational level, or other natural assets. While personal attention is time consuming, it can speed up a player's training progress.

Coaching Tips for Applying the Individualisation Principle

1. Set Clear Goals. Goals set for team results can be personalised according to position and players' abilities.

2. Test. Getting your baseline measurements and evaluation of results is the most precise way to apply this principle. In addition to fitness and skill testing, health-related tests performed by trainers and other professionals offer implications for how training can be adjusted.

3. Optimise Shortcomings. Devise ways to overcome weaknesses as much as possible. For example, for players with low motivation, set specific goals and reward progress. For example, those who naturally move slowly for whatever reasons, overload speed-related activities.

4. Gender Differences. Be sensitive to physical as well as cultural differences. Women have wider hips, a lower center of gravity, and carry more fat in certain areas than do men. Training tasks may need to be adjusted for these physical differences. Encourage and support girls and women equally with boys and men, particularly where a sport may be more accepted for one gender.

5. Positive-negative-positive. When offering coaching feedback, reinforce the good points, and also point out areas for improvement. This is especially helpful when a player has difficulty, whether on a given day or consistently due to personal weaknesses, positive reinforcement encourages him/her to persist.

6. Senior Cricketers. Older adults may need specific attention compared to younger players. Coaches should be sensitive to decreased flexibility, postural deviations, body composition, and other orthopedically-related factors. Adults prefer to be active participants in developing training programmes.

7. Youth Cricketers. Competitive youth cricket subjects children to many opportunities, as well as many physical and psychological vulnerabilities. Positive early experiences marked with success can lead the way to healthy lifetime habits.

Coaches and parents should accommodate such factors as; stage of learning, level of perceptual-motor development, and fitness level and capabilities. Children need acceptance and encouragement whether they win or lose.

THE TRANSFER PRINCIPLE

The Transfer Principle suggests that learning and performing one activity affects the performance of related skills and activities. This principle is essential for designing practice strategies that have the greatest positive impact on competitive performance. Correctly applying this principle saves valuable training time while accelerating results.

Coaching Tips for Applying the Transfer Principle

1. Identify similarities between previously learned skills and new skills.

2. Maximise the similarity between training activities and competitive conditions. Simulate various elements of competition (e.g. arousal level, game intensity, spectator noise) occasionally during training sessions, particularly during the in-season.

3. Provide adequate experience with fundamental skills before advancing to more complex skills. Well learned lead-up skills can positively influence a cricketer's performance in more demanding conditions at the next level of play (e.g., nets to centre wicket practice).

4. Develop more general capabilities, such as critical gross motor skills, that are adaptable to a variety of sport tasks. For example, in basketball, the vertical jump is a key element of rebounding and blocking shots.

5. Point out to the player how training activities will improve sport performance. For example, call attention to the balance, the hip drive and rotation, and the body movement in certain positions when teaching the bowling action.

THE SPECIFICS PRINCIPLE

The Specifics Principle is key to developing effective fitness training programs for cricket. Specifics also underlies how fast bowlers learn skills. However, the principle is sometimes misinterpreted.

Specifics and Sports Fitness

Specifics refers to the type of changes the body makes in response to training.

Very simply - **what you do is what you get.**

When a fast bowler trains, he or she repeatedly performs activities to prepare for the exact requirements of bowling fast. In time, the bowler's body becomes better able to meet the demands of bowling fast as it adapts to the training regimen.

Adaptations to training are most evident in elite fast bowlers. For example, the effects of years of rigorous training clearly distinguish the bodies of distance runners from fast bowlers, as a comparison.

For distance runners, major adaptations from the demands of sustained running include a larger, stronger heart and increased blood vessels to supply oxygen to the specific muscles involved in running. In contrast, adaptations to training for fast bowlers include increased size and thickness of specific muscles of the body that are trained to improve explosive power.

This principle applied to fitness training means that the overall energy demands of fast bowling determine which fitness components (e.g., strength, power, endurance) should be developed so that the requirements of the sport are matched.

For example, basketball fitness training should include some distance work with intermittent speed and agility training. In contrast, golfers would require little distance work, but train for power and flexibility. Fast bowlers require speed, power, balance, explosive energy, flexibility and endurance to enhance their technical skills and tactical expertise.

Specifics and Cricket Skill Learning

Skills are unique to each sport. Cricket requires fast bowlers to command an arsenal of options for executing skills so that they can make split-second adjustments in a variety of competitive situations.

Specifics for learning fast bowling skills involves performing a variety of closely related movements. Rather than practicing and perfecting any single skill or movement only, specifics of skill learning means that fast bowlers must develop variations of skills so that they can quickly adapt to the different conditions they will encounter in game play.

Early in learning, a bowler will tend to benefit from practicing skills with little variation because they are just beginning to understand what the skill requires. This is called the **cognitive** or **mental stage**. However, as learners progress, adding variation to practice better matches the specific demands of competition.

THE RECOVERY PRINCIPLE

The Recovery Principle dictates that fast bowlers need adequate time to recuperate from training and competition. Many believe that a fast bowler's ability to recover from workouts is just as important as the workout itself.

It is during rest periods that a fast bowler's body adapts to the stress placed upon it during intense workout sessions and competitions. Rest also provides time for a mental preparation and reflection.

The Recovery Principle applies both to immediate rest needed between bouts of exercise, as well as to longer time intervals of several hours to about two days.

When you sprint as fast as possible or lift heavy weights, you will notice that your heart still pumps hard and you breathe heavy for a while after you stop. The term "metabolic recovery" describes what takes place after you exercise, and it involves the post-exercise elevation of your metabolic rate or oxygen consumption.

Exercise intensity more profoundly affects recovery than does the duration of exercise. Maximising the recovery processes after interval training, weight training, or repeated sprint work is important.

Actively cooling down by jogging or walking immediately after intense exercise prevents the potential for venous pooling. Rhythmic exercise increases blood flow through the veins and heart during recovery, speeding up lactate removal from the blood.

Active recovery consisting of light-to-moderate cardio activity decreases blood lactic acid significantly faster than complete rest or passive recovery. Whether cycling or running, activities should remain at about 30-60% of the lactic threshold level.

Activity during recovery also maintains circulation to the heart, liver, and inactive muscles that are able to use lactic acid to synthesise glycogen.

Sleep, proper nutrition, and healthy lifestyle habits after intensive training periods are critical if an athlete is to recuperate.

Recovery can also be facilitated by stretching after workouts. Whirlpools and massage can also help muscles rest and rebuild more quickly while minimising muscle soreness. Upright activity in water also assists with recovery.

THE REVERSIBILITY PRINCIPLE

The Reversibility Principle dictates that you will lose the effects of training when you stop working out. Conversely, it also means that detraining effects can be reversed when you resume training. In short, **If you don't use it, you lose it.**

While rest periods are necessary for recovery, extended rest intervals reduce physical fitness. The physiological effects of fitness training diminish over time, causing the body to revert back to its pretraining condition.

Detraining occurs within a relatively short time period after an athlete ceases to train. Only about 10% of strength is lost 8 weeks after training stops, but 30-40% of muscular endurance is lost during the same time period.

While studies report statistically significant losses of fitness, a fast bowler can usually feel the effects of missing workouts in a shorter period of time. Generally, they notice losses in endurance and conditioning more quickly than strength.

The Reversibility Principle Does *Not* Apply to Retaining Skills

Sport skills are retained for much longer periods of time. A skill once learned is never forgotten, especially if well learned.

Coordination appears to store in long-term motor memory and remains nearly perfect for decades, particularly for continuous skills (e.g., cycling, swimming). Over time, strength, endurance, and flexibility are lost, but fast bowlers remember how to execute sport skills and strategies.

The challenge often concerns regaining precise timing after detraining. In other words, the motor skill programs remain intact but the body's physical tools for executing the programmes become rusty and must be resharpened.

Coaching Tips on Applying the Reversibility Principle

1. Conditioning. After long rest intervals, begin a conditioning programme to rebuild cricket fitness. After several weeks of detraining due to illness or for other reasons, a cricketer may need to increase training volume and reduce intensity to regain general conditioning.

2. Active Rests.   During the off season, active participation in other sports or activities minimises detraining effects and can even facilitate skill learning. Avoid long rest periods with complete inactivity.

3. Retraining. Increase exercise gradually and progressively after long periods of inactivity. Fast bowlers should avoid performing intense work without first reconditioning. (See the Overload Principle.)

4. Avoid Maximum Attempts. A fast bowler should not attempt to lift single maximum weight loads early in conditioning. They will remember how to properly execute the lifts, but may sustain an injury if they overestimate how much weight they can lift compared to their peak performance.

5. Flexibility. Emphasise stretching exercises to regain joint flexibility. This is particularly important for older adults who participate in senior cricket.

THE VARIATION PRINCIPLE

The Variation Principle suggests that minor changes in training regimens yield more consistent gains in sport performance. Training programs for virtually every sport include variations in intensity, duration, volume, and other important aspects of practice.

The most well known method of practice variability concerns training in phases. Typically, an annual cricket training programme includes phases of training for conditioning, intensive sport-specific work, in-season maintenance, and an off-season regimen. Training in phases, or periods, is called periodisation.

Periodisation was used by Eastern Europeans for about 50 years. Macrocycles (a year), mesocycles (about a month), and microcycles (a week) include planned changes in exercises, intensity, volume, and other training variables that target the athlete's goals for peaking during the competitive season.

Adjustments in training are very effective when used for skill learning, as well as for fitness training.

This principle does not conflict with the Specifics and Overload Principles. Specifics is about how the fast bowler's body adapts to the type of training program used, and training should be similar to the demands of bowling fast. Practice variability simply suggests that players should not perform exactly the same regimen each day. It supports specifics because competitive conditions present different situations that demand slightly different responses. The Overload Principle implies that gradual and progressive changes in training must occur in order for improvement to take place.

Training Tips for Applying the Variation Principle

1. **Set up an annual sports training plan** using phases, each with a specific purpose.

2. **Plan how all cricket training activities can cohesively build** to a training peak during the competitive season.

3. **In each week of each training phase, coordinate the intensity** of fitness training activities with technical and tactical work to allow ample recovery.

4. **For weight training,** adjust exercises, sets, reps, rest, and volume within a range that fits the training cycle.

5. **For aerobic training**, adjust distance, speed, duration, recovery, and volume within the training cycle.

6. **When signs of overtraining occur**, change workouts by reducing intensity and allowing longer recovery time.

CONCLUSION

I hope the above helps. The bottom line is you are completely responsible for your own career and pathway. And it is for you to **seek the answers you want** by finding out the right information. Do not look at what someone else does and try to copy them in training. That's because they might be fitter/better/younger than you or on a completely different training pathway. It is always best to seek the advice of a trusted health care professional before you embark on any training regime and I would strongly advise you work with an expert in Strength & Conditioning who can guide you safely to where you want to go.

14

Final Thoughts

Let's be honest here. You are not going to change a bowler's action or make tweaks to his positioning at the crease if you ask him to come charging in from a full run up, with a ball in his hand bowling to a batsman. The reason? He's only focusing on the outcome. But technique changes are part of the process. So you'll have to be smart about changing that.

Processes create outcomes. What you get in a match is the result of how you do it. And that's why if you only ever focus on the end result, you'll never know how to make any technical changes that are worthwhile or long-lasting.

I often hear coaches say, "Bowlers deal in the currency of taking wickets". This is very true and no one can argue with that. But a poor coach fails to understand that if you keep doing the same things wrong, you'll keep getting the same results. In other words, your 'currency' or at least your wealth of wickets can be dramatically improved by changing the process you use to get them.

It's no good just looking at the outcome and saying to a bowler, "you're bowling too short/full/down the leg side/too wide" without examining WHY he's doing that. Every outcome had a process – every effect has a cause.

The skill drills are thus designed to give you access to making changes to a bowler's action by helping them (and you) understand what should happen.

Here's a rough guide to how skill is learned:

1. Match situation – very little technical or process learned. Maximum experienced gained.

2. Nets – again very little learned technically as bowlers are thinking about batsman and where they are bowling

3. Bowling without a batter – good way to train in nets for a bowler as there are very few outcomes that can detract from experimenting

4. Bowling without a batter and a ball – this is the very best way to start doing

skill drills. There are no external influences, no penalties for a bad outcome, and no ball to worry about. In other words, this level of training is all about the bowler and their action.

You must strip out skill drills from nets and allow a bowler the opportunity to get it wrong. If you have a batsman thrashing away or hitting the ball, the bowler will only ever focus on the outcome – and the outcome doesn't matter in the slightest at this stage. So remove all external influences that can affect a bowler, which includes the ball itself. This type of bowling is called 'shadow bowling' and this lets a bowler 'bowl' many deliveries without a bad ball ever being bowled.

So now you've established the parameters for the drills, ensure the bowler does them at walking pace. Why? Because you want the bowler to be aware of what they're doing. And by walking things through the bowler will have to think about the drill in a way they do not think about their bowling. You are seeking to change a bowler's muscle memory, or ability to do the same thing repeatedly without conscious thought. And you will only make this change if the change is initially conscious.

Otherwise the bowler will merely go back to type. Their original software will take over and they will find change almost impossible or at least very hard. So change the environment, and slow everything down to the point they become aware of what they're doing.

It's at this point that you might find they even get it spectacularly wrong. I like sessions where bowlers get it wrong. Some of the best learning sessions are like this. It's challenging for the bowler and can lead to an even deeper level of understanding.

I have also worked with bowlers on drills with eyes closed.

Take the stumps away and have a bowler walk through their action to really feel what they're doing. Are they balanced? Or are they falling one way or the other? Where are their arms going, feet, head, legs? By closing eyes on walking drills, you can help a bowler tap into their emotion or kinaesthetic side. This is because when you lose one of your 5 major senses (vision) the others are temporarily heightened, and it's the feeling part we wish them to utilise.

It helps them to learn faster and change their muscle memory.

Once the drills have been done at a walking pace, build them up into a slow, gentle jog through drill. Timing will change and it becomes a challenge again. When they have mastered this, move to a run through drill. Again it will be a challenge.

Only when you are BOTH happy the action is what you want, then introduce the ball. Get them to hold it, but not let it go YET! By holding the ball part of their original muscle memory wants to take over, so don't let it. Drill it out. And when they have done this move to a ball release… let them bowl. But also know they will probably only be 50% of the drill, but hopefully 100% better than they were. And tell them not to worry WHERE the ball goes!

The secret is to get the bowler to do two things: experiment and exaggerate. This means try things to find out what works for them, and exaggerate the movements so the brain understands the changes by feel. That's all you can ask of a bowler who's doing skill drills.

Changing things a bowler has done for some time isn't easy. So be patient. Also, you won't 'break' someone's bowling action so don't worry about that. Too many coaches think they don't want to 'mess' with an action in case they break it. But let me tell you that however hard you work, after a session that bowler will go back to what they know. Therefore a bowler needs to do work in between sessions, which they cannot always do. It's what they do in between sessions that helps accelerate learning. The process of change starts when people think about change. And by working on things in between highly advanced technical sessions, they will move ahead faster.

Please tell the bowler and also understand yourself that while the drills are taking place, a bowler will probably go backwards in speed and accuracy or control. But you now know that these are outcomes and we are working on the processes. So it does not interest us in the slightest. That's why understanding what a skill drill is and what it achieves is vitally important. A skill drill is skill acquisition. You will change the timing and also the feeling of what comes as 'natural' for a bowler. They will experience a loss of timing and probably be out of their comfort zone. However, this is temporary. And with regular work on technique those changes start to become the new norm.

The time it takes to make changes permanent depends much on the individual. So get a bowler to agree to the changes (buy in) and help them to realise it will sometimes take them round a block in their action by going sideways or backwards.

Finally, the skill drills are designed to help a bowler to be as efficient as possible - and not perfect. We don't seek perfection but we are aiming for a bowler to become the best they can with what they have naturally. In other words, a bowler will adapt and adopt in the best way that suits them. These are tweaks to positioning and not action changes.

If a bowler does every skill drill perfectly well, they should have an outstanding action. So I put this to you. How many times have you seen someone with a Brett Lee or Dale Steyn action, playing 3rd team club cricket? None. That's because if you do those things that make you consistent and fast, you will migrate to the top naturally. So the drills are designed to help a bowler maximise their assets.

There are further developments in pace bowling coaching I am not able to share with you at this time because they are being worked on (trial & error, evidential proof) and are yet to be finalised. But rest-assured that there is some more good coaching stuff to come and improvements to coaching generically cannot be too far away one hopes, as fast bowling coaching catches up to the information that is available.

Simple things like training with a weighted cricket ball to help increase your arm speed, for instance, may become popular at some stage. I had some weighted balls specially made a few years ago and used them for those relevant muscle groups. Whilst you have to be careful not to alter your muscle memory and sequencing, they can work. Knowing what to do and what weight to use, is key.

One of the most important things for any cricketer, is to remain open-minded and inquisitive. The moment you stop questioning or thinking there might be something better to help you, is the time you cease to have the right mindset to stay ahead of the game.

Whatever level you play, you always want to be better and it is this approach to cricket that will look after you. The same is true for coaches who wish to improve their own knowledge regardless of the level they work at.

Be patient. Ask questions. Work hard. That ethos won't take you far wrong.

Finally, good luck. You can only control what is in your power and the rest is down to good fortune. So just make sure the part you can control is as good as you can make it.

Enjoy the ride.